SHETLAND

SHETLAND

NORMAN NEWTON

PEVENSEY

ISLAND GUIDES

The Pevensey Press is an imprint of
David & Charles plc

Copyright © Text and photographs
Norman Newton 1995

First published 1995

Map on page 6 by David Langworth

A catalogue record for this book is
available from the British Library.

ISBN 0 907115 95 0 (hardback)
ISBN 0 907115 88 8 (paperback)

Designed and typeset by
Drum & Company
and printed in Hong Kong by
Wing King Tong Co Ltd
for David & Charles
Brunel House   Newton Abbot
Devon

CONTENTS

Map of the island   6

1 Voes and Tombolos   7

2 Arriving on Mainland   27

3 Christians and Cliffs   35

4 A Castle, Causeways and a Bus   45

5 Walls and a Temple   56

6 Oil and Granite   62

7 Shetland's Northern Isles   72

8 Shetland's Remoter Islands   86

9 Walks and Excursions   92

Useful Information and Places to Visit   107

Place Names and their Interpretation   108

Further Reading   110

Index   111

Left: Near Greenbank, at the north end of Yell, with the cliffs of Unst in the distance

Half title: Muness castle, Unst

Title page: The settlement at Voe, at the head of Olna Firth

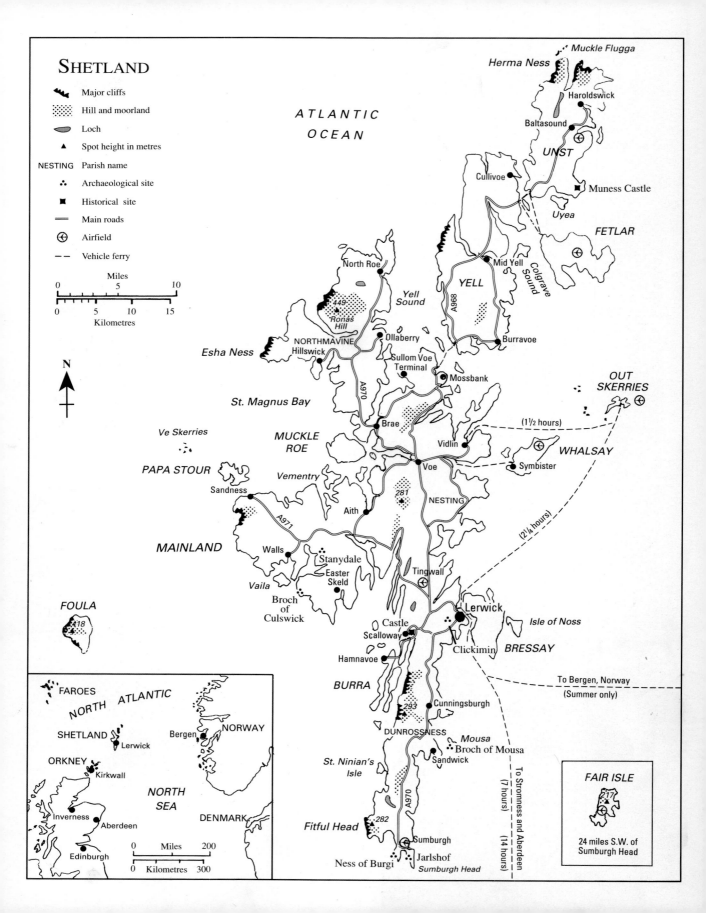

SHETLAND

- ◣ Major cliffs
- ⣿ Hill and moorland
- ⬯ Loch
- ▲ Spot height in metres
- NESTING Parish name
- ∴ Archaeological site
- ◼ Historical site
- ── Main roads
- ⊕ Airfield
- ─ ─ Vehicle ferry

Miles
0   5   10
Kilometres
0   5   10   15

N

ATLANTIC OCEAN

Muckle Flugga
Herma Ness
Haroldswick
Baltasound
UNST
Cullivoe
Muness Castle
Uyea
FETLAR

North Roe
Yell Sound
Mid Yell
YELL
Colgrave Sound
A968
Burravoe
▲ 449
'Ronas Hill'
NORTHMAVINE
Hillswick
Esha Ness
Ollaberry
Sullom Voe Terminal
Mossbank
OUT SKERRIES
St. Magnus Bay
A970
Brae
Vidlin
WHALSAY
Ve Skerries
MUCKLE ROE
Voe
Symbister
(1½ hours)
PAPA STOUR
Vementry
NESTING
Sandness
Aith
281
(2¼ hours)
MAINLAND
A971
Walls
Stanydale
Tingwall
Easter Skeld
Vaila
Broch of Culswick
Lerwick
Isle of Noss
FOULA
▲ 418
514
Castle
Scalloway
Clickimin
BRESSAY
Hamnavoe
BURRA
To Bergen, Norway
(Summer only)
293
Cunningsburgh
DUNROSSNESS
Mousa
Broch of Mousa
Sandwick
St. Ninian's Isle
A970
To Stromness and Aberdeen
(7 hours)
Fitful Head
282
Sumburgh
(14 hours)
Jarlshof
Ness of Burgi
Sumburgh Head

FAROES
NORTH ATLANTIC
SHETLAND
Lerwick
Bergen
NORWAY
ORKNEY
Kirkwall
NORTH SEA
DENMARK
Inverness
Aberdeen
Edinburgh

Miles
0   200
Kilometres
0   300

FAIR ISLE
▲ 217

24 miles S.W. of Sumburgh Head

1 VOES AND TOMBOLOS
An Introduction to Shetland

SHETLAND is quite different from any other part of the United Kingdom. It has a distinctive landscape, its very own dialect, a prosperous oil-based economy, an excellent integrated public transport system and a solid sense of community identity. It is not without its problems but, for an area perceived by the rest of Britain as being on the northern fringes of viable human settlement, Shetland is doing remarkably well.

Most people think of Shetland as lying in a box at the top of a map of the British Isles. This space-saving device is used by mapmakers because the distance from John O'Groats, on the north coast of mainland Scotland, to the northern extremity of the Shetland archipelago is about the same as the distance from John O'Groats to Edinburgh.

Shetland's capital, Lerwick, lies just north of latitude 60'N, so it is a lot closer to the Arctic Circle than to London. It lies just to the west of the Greenwich meridian, at 1' 9"W. The nearest point on the Scottish mainland is 93 miles (150km) to the south, while the ferry connection to Aberdeen is

A Russian scientific research vessel and Norwegian yachts in Lerwick's cosmopolitan harbour

A colourful welcome to Shetland at Lerwick's pier

This reproduction of a Viking galley takes tourists round Lerwick harbour: in the background are Lerwick's 'lodberries', eighteenth-century merchants' houses with a warehouse and pier attached

Glimpses of the harbour through winding streets remind the people of Lerwick of the importance of the sea in their lives

211 miles (340km), a journey taking the modern car ferries the best part of fourteen hours. Vehicles must check in at least an hour before sailing. Stromness, the port for Orkney, is eight hours sailing to the south. Both the Norwegian city of Bergen and the capital of the Faroe Islands, Torshavn, are about 250 miles (402km) from Lerwick.

The total land area of Shetland is 567 square miles (1,468 sq km), within a tortuous coastline of about 900 miles (1,450km). Nowhere on the many islands of Shetland is more than 3 miles (5km) from the sea.

Shetland's northerly latitude ensures long hours of daylight in the summer months and long hours of darkness in the winter. In May, June and July the twilight lasts far into the night, while on Midsummer Day there is very nearly seventeen and a half hours between sunrise and sunset. By contrast, the sunniest December day is barely five hours long. The seasons have a big impact on Shetland life and in the summer months people squeeze as much as possible into the long hours of daylight.

In Viking times Shetland was at the hub of Viking expansion: a base and staging post for raiders and settlers heading for the Faroes and Iceland to the north and west; Orkney and Caithness to the south; the Hebrides and Ireland to the south-west. The southerner's perspective of Shetland as being far away on the fringes of Europe will change after a few days in the cosmopolitan atmosphere of Lerwick. Shetland is still the hub of Nordic Europe, and still very much a part of Nordic culture, and proud of it.

POPULATION

OVER ONE HUNDRED ISLANDS make up the Shetland archipelago, ranging from the largest island, Mainland, to tiny uninhabited rocky skerries. Fifteen islands still support human populations – about 22,000 in all – of which about 8,000 live in the two neighbouring Mainland towns of Lerwick (7,220) and Scalloway (1,053). The west coast fishing port of Scalloway was once the Islands' capital, but in the last two centuries Lerwick, on the east coast of Mainland, has taken over that role.

Eighty per cent (17,000) of the 22,522 resident islanders live on Mainland (1991 Census figures) and the remainder of the population is scattered over surrounding small island communities, of which Muckle Roe, Trondra and Burra are now connected to Mainland by bridges or causeways.

POPULATION DISTRIBUTION

Mainland	17,651
Yell	1,083
Unst	1,067
Whalsay	1,043
Burra	886
Bressay	353
Trondra	117
Fetlar	87
Out Skerries	87
Fair Isle	68
Foula	45
Papa Stour	35
TOTAL	**22,522**

Mainland is naturally divided into several distinct areas. In the south, the peninsula of Dunrossness resembles a spear point and, indeed, one explanation of Shetland's name is that it derives from a Norse word for a spear. It runs as straight as an arrow for 20 miles (32km), but only 2–3 miles (around 4km) wide.

Lerwick, Scalloway and Tingwall occupy the central part of Mainland, while off to the west of Weisdale Voe is the district of Walls with its winding road ending at Sandness with a view of Papa Stour. Further north on Mainland are the districts of Nesting, Lunnasting and Delting: the -ting suffix indicates that these were administrative divisions in Norse times, when a 'ting' or local assembly, met in each area of Shetland.

At Brae, Mainland is almost cut in two at the isthmus of Mavis Grind. Rønas Voe divides the Esha Ness peninsula, pointing to the west, from the almost mountainous landscape of Rønas Hill and an area of bog

FROM SUMBURGH TO HERMANESS

The distances within Shetland are considerable and visitors will be surprised at how easy it is to accumulate huge mileages in a very short time. From Sumburgh Head, at the southern tip of Shetland, to Hermaness, at the north end of Unst, is a distance of about 70 miles (113km), with Muckle Flugga lighthouse perched on a further scrap of land just beyond that. To the south-west of Sumburgh Head, halfway to Orkney but administratively part of Shetland, is Fair Isle, 24 miles (39km) out in the northern ocean. Foula, 18 miles (29km) west of the Walls peninsula of Mainland, is also isolated from the main archipelago. All of the islands are well served by ferries and small aircraft.

Commercial Street in Lerwick is the commercial centre of the oldest part of the town

9

and dozens of small lochans to its north. The main road runs up the east coast of this northern part of Mainland to North Roe and Fedeland, where there are excellent and spectacular walks and impressive offshore natural arches and stacks.

Each of the islands of Shetland, and indeed each of the districts of Mainland, has its own charm and distinctive features, so there is no lack of variety for the visitor to explore.

ROCKS

THE DISTINCTIVE LANDSCAPE of Shetland is a result of changes in sea level after the end of the last Ice Age. About 10,000 years ago the sea level rose as the ice sheets melted, flooding river valleys which had been moulded over the preceding millennia. This accounts for the long, sinuous sounds or 'voes' which cut into the landscape bringing narrow tongues of water far inland from the open sea and forming narrow offshore islands, where folk now live on what were once the hilltops between neighbouring valleys. Weisdale Voe is perhaps the most scenically attractive; Sullom Voe the best known outside Shetland, as the site of Europe's largest oil and liquified gas terminal, commissioned in 1982 and averaging one million barrels of crude oil per day (see p 67).

Another recent geological feature, seen in many places around Shetland's coastline, are the sand and gravel spits connecting offshore islands to the shore. These are known to coastal geologists as 'tombolos', and are just as visually interesting in their own way as the dramatic cliff scenery which is also a feature of Shetland's coasts. One of the most beautiful is the tombolo which connects St Ninian's Isle to the Mainland, consisting of pristine, white shell sand, a fitting approach to Shetland's most holy site (see p 40).

Pages 10–11: A typical Shetland tombolo at Ness of Sound, West Yell

Left: Seabirds swirl like confetti in the wind currents around the cliffs of Noss, a nature reserve off the east side of Bressay

Below: Only two occupied houses now remain in the once thriving community of Lunnin, a remote but sheltered corner of Shetland's Mainland

SHETLAND'S LUCKY ESCAPE

In January 1993 the Braer oil tanker ran aground in the nearby Bay of Quendale and it seemed, for a while, that the beauty of St Ninian's Isle would be sullied, as an ecological disaster loomed. However, the Braer episode has been correctly described as 'the disaster which never happened'. A combination of good luck, and a fierce Atlantic storm, broke up the oil-slicks and minimised the damage. A year later, it was as if it had never happened. Shetland had a lucky escape, although the bad publicity did have an effect on tourism for a while.

Although the post-glacial features of the Shetland landscape give it its distinctive aspect, the underlying rocks are in fact, amongst the oldest in Europe, dating back 2,000 million years. The geology is complex and attracts visiting students and enthusiasts from far and wide. The island of Fetlar is a particular favourite. Although much of Shetland is relatively flat and low-lying, some parts are quite hilly: Rønas Hill, at the north end of Mainland, reaches an altitude of 1,477ft (450m). An access road leads to an abandoned military installation on the adjoining Collafirth Hill, from where there is a fine view and an opportunity to wonder at the weird reddish-pink granite landscape of this part of Shetland.

BIRDS

Oystercatchers nesting on the wall of Lunna Kirk

FOR MANY PEOPLE Shetland *means* birds and that is why they visit. A few days at the Fair Isle Bird Observatory and Lodge is every twitcher's ambition while serious ornithologists revel in the variety of species and the important research being carried out throughout Shetland. The islands are especially favoured for bird-watching as they lie at the southern limit of breeding for some Arctic species and are a seasonal crossroads for many migrating species. While the arrival of exotic species, blown well away from their normal track by autumnal gales, brings hundreds of enthusiasts with their telephoto lenses, most ornithologists come to see the gigantic colonies of seabirds, breeding in Shetland on a scale seen nowhere else in the British Isles.

There are seabird colonies all around the coastal cliffs of Shetland, with internationally important nature reserves at Hermaness and Noss, managed by Scottish Natural Heritage. The cliffs at Sumburgh Head, near the airport at the south tip of Mainland, are probably the most accessible by road. You can park your car below the lighthouse and peer over drystone walls at thousands of seabirds whirling like confetti around the cliffs, while puffins stand guard only a few feet away at the entrance to their burrows, tunnelled into the cliff-tops. The puffin is probably the most popular with visitors with its comical appearance and brightly coloured beak. Known in Shetland as the 'Tammie Norie', about 20 per cent of Scotland's puffins breed here. Guillemots and razorbills, other members of the auk family, also breed in massive numbers on cliff-ledges and crevices in the rocks.

Looking north-west from Lunnin across the Lunna peninsula

Away from the cliffs, the sight of gannets plunging into the sea from a great height is spectacular; their specially strengthened skulls make this possible. Other seabirds which breed in large numbers in Shetland include: kittiwakes; shags; cormorants and fulmars. Needless to say, visitors should not disturb breeding-sites, although Arctic terns, fulmars and skuas – or bonxies as they are called in Shetland – are quite capable of defending their territory effectively. More information on Shetland's birds can be found in many excellent small pamphlets available locally.

Thatching on one of the restored cottages at the Shetland Croft Museum

FLORA AND FAUNA

SHETLAND PONIES have been on the islands at least since Viking times. Although they can be seen throughout Shetland, and are superbly adapted to the environment and climate, there are not as many of them around as you might expect. In fact, the only native Shetland mammal is the otter which occurs in large numbers around the coasts. It is, however, a secretive animal and you may have to get up very early (or stay up very late) to see one. Hedgehogs, stoats, mountain hares, rabbits, field mice, house mice and brown rats are all thought to be introduced species.

Grey seals, which have a distinctive 'Roman nose' profile, and the smaller common seals, with a more 'dog-like' appearance, both inhabit the coasts while several species of whales and dolphins occur further offshore.

Botanists will find over eight-hundred species of flowering plants and ferns, including several subarctic or alpine species on Rønas Hill. Shetland has an undeserved reputation for being treeless and barren. In the spring and summer it is extremely colourful as there are small tree plantations in Weisdale and individual trees and shrubs in many gardens. The Shetland landscape is not naturally treeless at all, but has been made that way by centuries of grazing and farming, starting in prehistoric times. Peat, which is plentiful in moorland areas, shows that the islands were covered by a scrub woodland of birch, hazel and willow. A deterioration in climate at the end of the Bronze Age accelerated the deforestation processes started by Neolithic farmers and now completed in the last two centuries by sheep.

HISTORY

THE FIRST SHETLANDERS came to the islands soon after the melting of the ice sheets of the last Ice Age made them habitable again. The earliest colonists were hunter-gatherers who feasted on shellfish and picked berries to survive. At first, they may have stayed only seasonally – migrants – like many other species which visit these islands.

THE STONE AGE

Only in the Neolithic period did the first permanent settlers arrive. These Stone Age farmers cleared the land, made fields and enclosures, grew cereal crops and raised sheep and cattle. They lived in round houses, which now appear in the landscape as hut circles, and buried their dead in chambered cairns, which in Shetland are heel-shaped. The most important building surviving from this period is the 'temple', or more probably meeting house, at Stanydale, in the Walls district (see page 59).

THE BRONZE AGE

In the Bronze Age, by about 2000BC, a new culture arrived for the first time using metals for tools and jewellery. The most visible signs of their presence are the standing stones which dot the landscape, which some experts think may have been used for surprisingly complicated observations of the sun, moon and stars: essential for formulating a precise calendar. Less obvious, but more common, are the 'burnt mounds', probably Bronze Age cooking sites and the upland field systems, many covered now by peaty landscapes.

It was a deterioration in climate which brought the Bronze Age to an end in Shetland, disrupting agricultural practices and possibly undermining

Pages 16–17: The beautifully situated old Kirk of Lunna

Top left: Yachts from Norway celebrate their national day in Lerwick harbour

Bottom left: The bus station in Lerwick is the hub of the island's public transport system

The ferry from Bressay arriving at the Albert Buildings, once a coal merchant's office and store

their religion, if in fact it was based on eclipse prediction, as some students of standing stones have claimed. As the weather became colder and wetter, the scrub vegetation on the hillier parts of Shetland began to turn into peat (decayed plant remains) used extensively for fuel in recent centuries. In prehistoric millennia, Shetland culture and society was much more in tune with the rest of the British Isles than it is today. The same cultures built the same kinds of monuments, with slight regional variations, but a Bronze Age tourist travelling, say from Brittany to Shetland would have found the standing stones familiar.

THE IRON AGE

In the Iron Age, Shetland began to develop more distinctively. At first, its new arrivals brought with them the technology and building practices which exist all over northern Europe, particularly their liking for building hill forts, surrounded by ramparts and ditches. Gradually new forms of defence evolved, culminating in a technological breakthrough which some scholars believe may have been invented in Shetland: the broch.

These circular stone towers, up to 40ft (13m) high, were a feature of the Iron Age landscape in Shetland, Orkney, Caithness and Sutherland, and the Hebrides, with a scattering further south. Whether they originated in the Western Isles or in Shetland is an unresolved debate among archaeologists. However, one school of thought argues that because the broch on the island of Mousa is so complete, and so perfect, it represents the finest and best achievement of the broch-builders (see p39). On balance, it seems more likely that brochs did originate further south, perhaps on Skye. They first appeared around 200BC and by AD200 were no longer in use. Some, in a partially ruined state, evolved into a new form, the wheelhouse, also found in Orkney and the Western Isles.

EARLY CHRISTIANS

When the first Christian missionary-monks arrived in Shetland from Ireland, in the sixth century AD, they found the islands inhabited by Picts (as was the case in most of the rest of the northern half of what is now Scotland). Little is known of these people beyond their distinctive symbol stones, and metalwork, both of which can be admired in Shetland Museum. The Christian monks, who would have been Gaelic-speaking, established monastic communities on remote islands, but were wiped out by the arrival of the Vikings, around AD800.

THE VIKINGS

It was the Vikings who, more than any other culture, have left an enduring mark on Shetland. The Northern Isles were never settled by Gaels, apart from a few Irish monks unlike in the Hebrides where the missionaries were followed by thousands of settlers (see chapter 3). In the Viking period Shetland was ruled by the earldom established in Orkney in AD872 by the King of Norway and remained under Norse sovereignty even after the Treaty of Perth, in 1266, brought the Western Isles and all the Hebrides under Scottish control.

SCOTTISH CONTROL

In 1469 Shetland (and Orkney) were pledged to the Scottish crown as part of the dowry of Margaret, daughter of the King of Denmark, on the occasion of her marriage to the prince who was later to become James III of Scotland. It was anticipated that they would revert to Scandinavian rule when the debt was paid and a schedule of annual repayments was agreed. When this pledge was never redeemed, the islands remained under Scottish control. Some people believe that *sovereignty* over Shetland and Orkney still remains with the King of Norway but after such a long passage of time the claim has lapsed. However, this is a very live political issue in Shetland.

Lunna House, where Norwegian resistance fighters were trained during World War II and sent back home on the 'Shetland Bus'

Overleaf: The P&O ferry St Sunniva heading up the Sound of Bressay for the voyage to Aberdeen

In 1564 Mary, Queen of Scots, granted control of Orkney and Shetland to her half-brother, Robert Stewart, who commenced a harsh regime of tax collecting in order to maximise his income. His son, Patrick, pursued the same exploitative policies even more rigidly. It was he who built Scalloway Castle, in 1600, which then became his main residence and the centre of law and government in Shetland. He built equivalent palaces in Orkney.

GETTING THERE

THE MAIN FERRY SERVICE to Shetland is from Aberdeen in north-east Scotland to Lerwick, the capital of Shetland. The crossing, normally overnight, takes fourteen hours and is operated by P & O Scottish Ferries (tel 01595 4848). An alternative route goes from Aberdeen to Stromness, in Orkney, then on to Lerwick, taking eighteen hours. There is a car ferry from Scrabster on the north coast of Scotland near Thurso to Stromness, on Orkney, and some visitors use this route to add variety to a northern holiday. The passage time from Stromness to Lerwick is eight hours.

If your ultimate destination is not on Mainland Shetland, you can take one of the frequent inter-island car ferries operated by Shetland Islands Council. Each island has its own booking office but the Tourist Information Office in Lerwick has timetables and advice (tel 01595 3434).

If you elect to come to Shetland by air, there are scheduled services to Sumburgh Airport from Aberdeen and Inverness (via Orkney), operated by British Airways (tel 01950 60345). Small aircraft operate from Tingwall Airport near Lerwick to the outlying islands, including Fair Isle. Several companies operate car and minibus hire services and vehicles can be picked up and left at Sumburgh Airport.

Most people arriving at Sumburgh Airport arrive, not by fixed wing scheduled services, but by helicopter, from North Sea oil platforms. In 1992 185,474 helicopter passengers passed through Sumburgh, compared to 93,825 scheduled passengers. Another 163,000 arrived as charter passengers, almost all of them working in the oil industry. Scatsta airstrip, beside the Sullom Voe oil terminal, handled another 14,000 passengers.

If you don't arrive by ferry, aeroplane or helicopter, you may arrive by yacht – about 400 arrive in Lerwick every year – mainly from Scandinavia. The harbour often has a cosmopolitan air, with foreign fishing vessels from many European countries and gaily coloured yachts from Norway or other British yachting clubs.

However you choose to journey to Shetland, or indeed if you are just an armchair traveller, you will assuredly find these northern islands a fascinating and continually interesting destination, at any season of the year.

Right: Sunset at Lunnin on Shetland's Mainland

2 ARRIVING ON THE MAINLAND:
Lerwick's Lodberries and the Islands' Capital

LERWICK

LERWICK is Shetland's biggest town; administrative capital; main harbour; shopping centre; and almost one-third of the population live there. The old part of the harbour, now used predominantly by small boats, is colourful and picturesque and well sheltered by the island of Bressay to the east. The Norse name means 'muddy bay' but in the Middle Ages the shoreline was altered by merchants and traders and turned into a waterfront of houses and warehouses, a few of which survive. These are known as 'lodberries', the piers built by merchants so that goods could be loaded and unloaded directly from their own warehouses. Dutch traders followed their herring fishing fleet and, by the end of the seventeenth century, Lerwick had grown to a town of around 700, making it a competitor to the existing island capital at Scalloway. It is now surrounded by the houses and streets of the expanding town.

The ramparts of Fort Charlotte were built in 1665 in the face of a perceived threat from Holland during the second Dutch War and today overlooks the Bressay ferry pier. It takes its name from George III's queen, Charlotte.

By the middle of the nineteenth century the town of Lerwick had grown to over 3,000 and assumed the role of the principle administrative centre. At the end of the century the population was approaching 5,000 and today is over 7,000. Many impressive public buildings were built in Victorian Shetland such as the Town Hall, built in 1882, of Bressay sandstone.

Left: A street scene in the town centre of Lerwick

The library and museum in Lerwick: one of the cultural centres of the island

RELICS AND READING

*Near the Town Hall is the Shetland
Library and Museum building
which houses the treasures of
Shetland's historical and printed
heritage. The museum, situated
above the library, reflects the
importance of the sea and shipping
in Shetland's history. However, the
archaeological collections are
outstanding, reflecting the quality of
the prehistoric sites throughout the
islands. Pride of place though must
go to the St Ninian's Isle treasure –
or at least a replica of the hoard of
Pictish silver dating from Early
Christian times – discovered in
1958. The originals are in
Edinburgh, in the Royal Museum of
Scotland, but the replicas are
exceptionally well done.*

*Shetland Library caters for all
the reading requirements of today's
residents but also acts as a
repository of an outstanding
collection of books on the history
and culture of the Shetland Islands.
The Shetland Room is a treasure
house of local history material,
including local newspapers, and, in
combination with the material in
the Shetland Archives, provides
everything necessary for research
into the islands' past.*

*Top and bottom right: Clickimin broch,
on the outskirts of Lerwick, an imposing
Iron Age stone tower built 2,000 years
ago. It is easily accessible and a good
introduction to Shetland's prehistory*

Inside, stained-glass windows depict episodes from Shetland's history. The County Buildings and Anderson High School both date from this period.

On the southern edge of Lerwick is its oldest building, Clickimin broch, dating from the Iron Age. Once a much higher stone tower, of the type best seen on the island of Mousa, the broch of Clickimin, excavated in the 1950s, greatly added to our understanding of the past. The remains of several periods of building can be found there, but the broch tower would have been the most spectacular. These remains are in the care of the Secretary of State for Scotland and are well interpreted with information boards and a guidebook. Originally they stood on a small island connected to the shore of the loch by a causeway. The level of the loch has fallen, combined with silting, making the site accessible. Nearby is Clickimin Leisure Centre, opened in 1985, providing excellent sports and recreational facilities. It is also a venue for concerts and other functions.

On the other side of Lerwick the shore has been transformed by recent industrial developments particularly associated with the oil industry. This is also the site of the Islands' main power station, and of the Holmsgarth ferry terminal, where the P & O ferries come and go. Now somewhat over-whelmed by these developments is a lovely little eighteenth-century building, the Böd of Gremista. The böd, or fishing booth, has been restored as a museum of the fishing industry. One room is devoted to Arthur Anderson (1791–1868), a founder of the Peninsular and Oriental Steam Navigation Company, who was born in this house.

This part of Lerwick is the one place in Shetland where the activities of the oil industry intrude into the landscape to any great extent. Even at Sullom Voe, the largest oil and gas terminal in Europe, careful planning has minimised the effect and the installation seems to blend with the landscape. This is not the case in Lerwick. It is impossible to exaggerate the importance of oil in the Shetland economy. It has transformed the islands in many ways, most of them for the benefit of the communities. Most obvious to visitors are the excellent roads which make travel around so much easier than previously and the excellent inter-island ferries, which minimise the incon-venience of living on one of the outlying islands.

There are other ways in which Shetland has benefitted from oil. Almost every island and community of any size has a new community centre and swimming pool: there is one pool for every 2,000 people in Shetland. These new facilities, and the excellent transport network, are immediately obvious to mainland Scots who find none of these advantages in the Hebrides, or even in some of the remoter parts of the Highlands. The ways in which the Shetland Islands Council negotiated with oil companies, and arranged for financial compensation for the disruption this industry brought, are much admired in other parts of Scotland.

There are lots of things to do and see in Lerwick. There is a summer exhibition of island life at Isleburgh House, itself an impressive building, and demonstrations of traditional arts and crafts are of particular interest to

visitors. The Up Helly Aa exhibition in St Sunniva Street explains the history of Shetland's annual fire festival. Each community in turn builds a replica Viking longship which is consumed in flames each January in Lerwick harbour, amid much jollity, as a celebration of the end of winter. Although this festival was the creation of Victorian romanticism and nostalgia, it draws on many elements of Shetland's past and is now a central event in island life. It is very much an event enjoyed to the fullest by Shetlanders themselves for, although it does attract some tourist interest, January is hardly the time to promote tourism. The centrepiece of the Up Helly Aa exhibition is a Viking galley, a full-size replica of a Viking longship. If you want to experience what it was like to be a Viking raider you can take a trip around Lerwick harbour on summer evenings in the *Dim Riv*, a 40ft (12m) replica of a traditional Viking longship.

At the core of Lerwick's townscape is Commercial Street, from which narrow alleys and lanes run uphill to Hillhead and the main residential areas of the town and downhill to the harbour. Commercial Street is paved in traditional fashion and has restricted access for vehicles: there is an enormous car park at the harbour nearby. For visitors, the centrepiece of Commercial Street is the Tourist Information Centre, near the Market Cross (tel 01595 3434). Here you can get all sorts of information about practically *anything* going on *anywhere* in Shetland, some of it in the form of information sheets and leaflets on walks, birds, archaeology, crafts, activities of all kinds from windsurfing to pony-trekking, and lots more. They also stock all the maps you are likely to need.

Just up the road, at the *Shetland Times* bookshop, you will find a tremendous selection of books on Shetland. There are several excellent photographers working in Shetland and their work appears in various calendars and postcards, as well as in framed enlargements.

All along Commercial Street, and on the waterfront and its adjoining lanes, there are all manner of shops. Some are very old fashioned, while others sell the most up-to-date clothes or technological wizardry. On the edges of Lerwick are the inevitable supermarket, petrol stations and even a shopping centre. As almost everything sold in Lerwick has come from Aberdeen, and further afield, on the ferries the prices are surprisingly reasonable, though often recognisably higher than on the Scottish mainland. This is a problem that Shetland shares with all island communities but it is more fortunate than most in having a large enough population who are able to produce goods and services locally. Shetland lamb, and locally available fish, are particularly good.

Lerwick has grown up on a small peninsula, and on its southerly point, the Knab, there is an excellent viewing point. This is where photographers come to snap ships coming and going from Lerwick harbour, with Bressay Lighthouse in the background promising an interesting composition. The park here, near Anderson High School, is a popular spot for an evening stroll.

PINTS AND PERFORMANCES

Another feature of Lerwick town centre is the number of pubs and hotels, some of which are renowned for impromptu music sessions. Shetland has a long tradition of its own style of fiddle music and you can often drop in on 'performances' which would command large audiences in the outside world. All year round there are lots of entertainments, not just in Lerwick, but in halls and community centres throughout the islands. Shetland life is certainly not boring and this is one way of combating the sometimes rather grim winter weather and long hours of winter darkness. In the summer months, read the Shetland Times or listen to the local radio station to find out what's on, there is always an impressive selection to choose from.

A fishy detail on a lamppost outside the Town Hall in Lerwick
Left: The Queen's Hotel, Lerwick, one of Shetland's oldest hostelries

The Bressay ferry loading at Lerwick for one of its frequent crossings

NOSS

Just to the east of Bressay is the tiny island of Noss, which has been a National Nature Reserve since 1955 because of its important seabird colonies. It can only be visited between May and August, when a warden is present. The Noup of Noss is an ideal place for bird-watching and it is possible to buy leaflets explaining the history and natural environment of this interesting little island. It takes about three hours to explore the island properly. The main house, at Gungstie, is occupied by a Scottish Natural Heritage warden and staff during the summer but otherwise Noss is uninhabited (except for the thousands and thousands of seabirds). Gungstie House was built in the seventeenth century and has a small visitor information room. The Marquis of Londonderry kept his Shetland pony stallions in the outbuildings here at the end of the nineteenth century, breeding ponies for work in his coal-mines in Durham.

BRESSAY

THE ISLAND OF BRESSAY protects Lerwick from easterly winds while Bressay Sound provides sheltered waters for shipping. Bressay is a small island supporting a small population most of whom work in Lerwick or in oil-related industries. It is only 7 miles (11km) from north to south and only 3 miles (5km) across, reached by a frequent ferry service from Lerwick. The current population is just over 300 but in the 1841 Census over 900 lived on Bressay, most of them in crofting townships cleared for sheep farms later in the nineteenth century.

At Gunnista, at the north end of Bressay, the ruins of the medieval church of St Olaf are worth a visit, and it's an easy walk from the ferry pier over the island to St Mary's church, a cruciform ruin built on the site of an earlier chapel. A Pictish symbol stone from here is in the Shetland Museum in Lerwick. On the west side of Bressay, facing Lerwick, there are the remains of several factories once used in herring processing, when herring was the mainstay of the Shetland economy. From the 1930s this fishery collapsed, for reasons still not completely understood, which in a period of economic recession caused much hardship in Shetland as in other parts of Scotland dependent on this industry. A modern fishmeal factory at Heogan maintains Bressay's tradition of fish-processing.

Geologically, Bressay is composed of old red sandstone, and the cliffs on the south coast, especially at the Ord and at Bard Head, are impressive. There is a fine panoramic view from the top of Ward Hill (742ft; 226m).

Left: The Lerwick lifeboat on exercise in Bressay Sound

3 CHRISTIANS AND CLIFFS:
South Mainland and the Dunrossness Peninsula

ROM LERWICK to Sumburgh Head a long finger of land points to the south, crammed with history, archaeology, stunning scenery and interesting attractions. The west side of this peninsula is sparsely populated, but there are thriving communities all along the more sheltered eastern side, some of them densely settled townships, at least by Shetland standards. Gulberwick, Quarff, Cunningsburgh and Sandwick between them have a population of over 1,700, while the southern part of the peninsula has another 1,500 people, giving a total of 3,200 Shetlanders, or over 14 per cent of the total, living on the Mainland south of Lerwick.

The broch of Mousa is built from the flagstone found on the foreshore nearby, without mortar, of drystone construction throughout

Left: Sand Lodge, Sandwick, is a fine example of the large mansion houses scattered throughout Shetland

Overleaf: The Sandwick area is the departure point for the island of Mousa, with its broch

The broch of Mousa is the most complete example in Scotland, surviving to almost its full height – an impressive Iron Age monument

GULBERWICK

Gulberwick has the distinction of appearing in the *Orkneyinga Saga*, the Norse history of the Northern Isles and the Hebrides which is one of our major sources for understanding the Viking period. Earl Rognvald was shipwrecked here in 1148, though we do not know if it was his silver brooch which was found here and can now be seen in the Shetland Museum.

FLADDABISTER

At Fladdabister there are the ruins of two lime kilns where the local limestone, which produces such fertility and such a profusion of wild flowers, was burnt in layers of peat to produce lime ash, which was used as a fertiliser and also in building mortar.

MAIL

Just south of Cunningsburgh, in the small cemetery at Mail, an extremely important Pictish stone was discovered in 1993. The Mail Stone, now in the Shetland Museum, depicts a Pictish warrior with battleaxe and club, but with a dog's head.

This part of Shetland has a far higher density of archaeological monuments than other districts showing that its more favourable environment was apparent in prehistoric times. Three of the historic sites, the broch at Mousa, the prehistoric village at Jarlshof and the Christian settlement on St Ninian's Isle, are of outstanding national and indeed international importance.

Moving south down the peninsula, past Mail, the main road cuts inland skirting the district of Sandwick, a populous and fertile corner of Shetland. The big house in Sandwick, Sand Lodge, has a seventeenth-century core with many additions. From the nearby slipway a summer boat service takes visitors across to the island of Mousa.

DUNROSSNESS

From Levenwick the main road runs down the middle of the peninsula entering Dunrossness parish. On the high hill above the main road are communications dishes, part of a network linking North Sea oil rigs. At Boddam signs indicate the Shetland Croft House Museum: a house, steading (farmstead) and water mill typical of a mid-nineteenth century croft. Inside, the furnishings are authentic and give an excellent idea of what life was like. A leaflet explains the detail of life on the croft and an attempt has been made, in the surrounding fields, to recreate farming practices of the period.

The farming year began on the croft in late March when the corn rigs were manured and then ploughed. In small patches of land where ploughing with a horse was not feasible ploughing was done laboriously by hand. In the middle of April potatoes were planted and then peats were cut for winter fuel and left to dry in the summer sun.

MOUSA

The broch of Mousa (left) is the finest example of a type of prehistoric fortress which is unique to Scotland. The characteristic feature of these drystone towers is the hollow-wall construction with mural galleries allowing access to the space between the inner and outer skins of the wall, connected inside the wall with stone stairs. There are over five hundred brochs in Scotland concentrated in Shetland, Orkney, Caithness, Sutherland and the Western Isles. Almost all are collapsed mounds of rubble. A few survive to something approaching their full height but only Mousa is complete. Perhaps its isolation prevented it from being robbed for building rubble, coupled with a large element of luck.

At Mousa the broch has a diameter of 50ft (15m) and is complete to a height of 43.5ft (13.3m). The only entrance is at ground level facing the sea, through a passage protected by a door halfway along. Inside the wall it is possible to ascend to the top of the tower up stone staircases. The view from the top is well worth the effort. The broch was handed over to the state for protection as an Ancient Monument in 1885 by John Bruce of Sumburgh and in 1919 was cleared of debris and consolidated.

There is the shell of a hall house or Haa, built in the late eighteenth century. There are also burnt mounds and, on the west side of the island, sandy beaches and seals. The boat trips from Sandwick are arranged to allow ample time to explore the broch and enjoy a walk across the island: this trip is highly recommended and for many visitors will be the highlight of their Shetland holiday.

BIGTON AND
ST NINIAN'S ISLE

*Between Levenwick and Boddam a
loop road crosses the peninsula to
the west side to the village of Bigton
which overlooks St Ninian's Isle.
Here is another of Shetland's most
important historical sites. St Ninian
was an Early Christian saint whose
main monastery was at Whithorn
in Wigtownshire, right at the other
end of Scotland. He was the first
Christian missionary to travel into
northern Scotland, or Pictland as it
was then. Ninian died in AD422.
The monastery he established in
Shetland is in a beautiful location
on a small island connected to the
mainland by a tombolo of white
shell sand. The ruins of a twelfth-
century church lie over an earlier
chapel. Inside this building, under a
slab, a hoard of Pictish silver was
discovered in 1958. It may have
been buried around AD800 when
Viking raids began. The originals
are in Edinburgh, in the Royal
Museum of Scotland, with replicas
in Lerwick. A leaflet describing this
important find is widely available in
Shetland.*

Cattle were kept in the steadings during the long winter and let out in
the spring when there was grass available. Haymaking started in July and the
hay was stored in the yard in haystacks. Oats and barley were cut with sickles
by mid-September and, after drying in stooks, were stored in stacks in the
farmyard. In mid-October the potatoes were harvested and stored in the
barn. The sheaves of grain were threshed and the grain dried in a kiln. Peats
were stacked and fish and meat prepared for the winter. Each crofter tried
to be self-sufficient and self-reliant.

Many crofters also worked as fishermen. In Dunrossness every croft
would have a yoal; a small, fast, perfectly designed little boat which was used
to keep the families supplied with fresh fish. Sometimes they provided a little

extra by way of a cash income, fishing for saithe in the summer. Fish was the major part of the crofter's diet and, although the life was dreadfully hard and unpredictable to the point of being precarious, the diet was healthy enough. Many Shetlanders emigrated in search of a better life or travelled the seven seas as mariners and adventurers. Almost every Shetland croft could be sure of having the long winter nights made more entertaining with stories of foreign travel, and the young boys must have wondered when they would get their chance to travel in the wider world. The Croft House Museum encourages such thoughts and speculations and gives us an insight into the life of our predecessors and ancestors which no books can ever hope to achieve.

The prehistoric village of Jarlshof and Sumburgh Hotel at the south end of the Dunrossness peninsula

41

JARLSHOF

The archaeological remains at Jarlshof came to light in 1905, revealed in a storm in similar circumstances to the equally significant prehistoric village of Skara Brae, Orkney. Subsequent excavations showed Neolithic occupation; successive Bronze Age levels with intact houses; an Iron Age broch; followed by a later wheelhouse; Pictish houses and a medieval Norse village. The site is well presented, with walkways and viewpoints, and constant injunctions for visitors not to walk on the walls. There are good interpretative panels and a small guidebook can be purchased from the site office where there is also a small display and museum. All in all, Jarlshof is a wonderful place. Over the centuries much has been lost to the sea but the storms which have destroyed so much of the site have also revealed what is left to admire.

THE LOCH OF SPIGGIE

The Bigton loop road continues past the Loch of Spiggie which is an important nature reserve. It is the largest loch in the southern half of Shetland and of national importance as a wildfowl reserve. The loch is an important refuge for whooper swans which breed in Iceland and come to Spiggie in late September. By November there can be over three hundred present but, as the water level of the loch rises and as their food supply becomes depleted, most of them move further south to sites in southern Scotland and Ireland. However, about forty swans stay throughout the winter, feeding on the surrounding pastures and on nearby lochs.

Several breeds of duck also frequent the Loch of Spiggie especially goldeneye, pochard and tufted duck – over 150 of each is normal. In the spring, long-tailed ducks arrive, moult into summer plumage, and head off in May to their Arctic breeding grounds, Numerous other species can be seen throughout the summer months. There are good views of the loch from the public road which runs down its west side and around the northern end.

Just to the south of the loch is Quendale, where a large nineteenth-century water mill has been restored. At the Bay of Quendale environmental damage from the *Braer* disaster has all but vanished.

SUMBURGH HEAD

One of the most interesting parts of Shetland is to be found right at the southern tip of the Dunrossness peninsula. Sumburgh Head, with its lighthouse and bird-cliffs, Sumburgh Airport and the Jarlshof settlement, make this one of the most popular areas for visitors.

The lighthouse on Sumburgh Head was built in 1821 by Robert Stevenson. Now automated, it was Shetland's first lighthouse. This is an excellent area to view seabirds on the precipitous cliffs. At the airport, the new Wilsness Terminal, a geometric concrete structure, was opened in 1979 with the requirements of the oil industry in mind. It contrasts starkly with its environment but suits its purpose well and seems architecturally appropriate.

Sumburgh Hotel was built in baronial style as a mansion house for the Bruce family in 1867. Guest wings were added in 1897 and modern bedroom blocks in the seventies. Architecturally it is far more out of place in the landscape than the air terminal particularly as the modern additions do not exactly blend in with the baronial original.

Just beside the hotel is one of Europe's premier archaeological sites, Jarlshof. The most visible building is the sixteenth-century Old House of Sumburgh, built as the residence of Robert Stewart who was granted the Lordship of the Northern Isles in 1564. William Bruce, who came to Shetland to the tenancy of Sumburgh in 1592, used it as the family home, until the seventeenth century when it was superseded by Sumburgh Farm-

house. The name Jarlshof was invented by Sir Walter Scott for the medieval farmhouse in his novel *The Pirate*, but now applies to the whole site.

It is not unusual for Bronze Age house sites to survive – we usually refer to them as hut-circles – and they are a feature of upland Britain from the north of Scotland to the south of England. But, it is unusual, if not unique for an entire village to be discovered. From the remains at Jarlshof we can see that the Bronze Age people lived in small, circular houses or huts with stone walls and thatched roofs and a cooking hearth in the middle. The houses were built side by side, with space in between for primitive streets. It must have been a busy, crowded settlement with little privacy and with every-body's effort directed towards communal survival. Even so, there must have been a ruling élite and, perhaps, a priestly class who looked after the village's rituals and planned the next ceremony at the nearest standing stone.

Although the prehistoric houses are remarkable, the centrepiece of Jarlshof is the longhouse built by the first Norse settlers. The stone founda-tions survive, with slightly bowed side walls, but the turf walls and heather thatch roof have long decayed. The Norse period was easily the most influential in the history of Shetland and five hundred years after the collapse of Norse sovereignty the effects of their occupation of Shetland still pervade every aspect of Shetland life. Many visitors have commented on the

People have lived in Jarlshof for over eight thousand years: these Bronze Age houses are a well-preserved example of a prehistoric village

An Iron Age wheelhouse at Jarlshof, much altered and rebuilt, but a fine example of a class of monument found throughout the northern isles

The medieval hall of Jarlshof which features in the work of Sir Walter Scott

fact that parts of Shetland *look* Scandinavian. It is clear that the Viking settlers liked it there and quickly made themselves at home. Back in Norway, around AD1000, there was a small population explosion and great pressure on cultivable land so emigration was encouraged. Orkney became their local administrative headquarters but Shetland was saturated with Norse settlers too. The Northern Isles were used as a staging post, from where summer raiders set out for the Western Isles of Scotland and, particularly, Ireland where the rich pickings of Christian monasteries were a great attraction. Norse raiding expeditions, south along the coasts of Scotland and the Irish Sea, were a continuing activity until the thirteenth century and were only brought to an end with the political transfer of the former Norwegian possessions to the Scottish state.

However, even after the transfer of sovereignty, Norse customs continued to dominate Shetland life despite the imposition of Scottish lairds. Even today, it is clear that native Shetlanders feel a tremendous sense of community identity as Shetlanders which is a much more potent force in their lives than their 'Scottishness'. This remains true despite a much needed influx of outsiders into the population with the expansion of the oil industry which, if anything, has brought Shetlanders together in the common purpose of maximising the benefits to be gained from this new wealth. As new technology allows exploration in deeper and deeper water, especially to the west of Shetland, this new lynchpin in the Shetland economy seems to ensure stable prosperity well into the next century.

4 A CASTLE, CAUSEWAYS AND A BUS:
Scalloway and Burra Isle

SCALLOWAY

Above: The castle and harbour at Scalloway, once more important than the current capital at Lerwick. Below: modern developments at Scalloway harbour reflect the importance of the fishing industry in Shetland's economy

O NLY 5 MILES (8km) to the west of Lerwick, on the west side of Mainland but another world away, lies the medieval capital of Shetland, Scalloway. With a population of just over 1,000, Scalloway is the second largest town in Shetland, after Lerwick. The name comes from the Norse *Skalavagr* meaning 'the bay of the Skali' (hall). Scalloway is at the focus of an historic area of Shetland with Norse sites at Tingwall and Loch Strom close by.

Until the eighteenth century Scalloway was the prosperous capital of Shetland and although most administrative functions, including the law courts were moved to Lerwick, Scalloway continued to prosper from the fishing industry in the nineteenth century. There is still a fishing fleet based here and in recent years harbour improvements, and a marina, seem to have ensured the town's future as a port. If oil exploration to the west of Shetland becomes as important as the planners hope, some of Scalloway's historic prosperity may return.

45

There are some attractive buildings in Scalloway some of which, particularly on the old waterfront, are being renovated. Blackness Pier, near the castle, was originally built around 1830 in connection with the export of salt cod to Spain. It was extended, in 1896, to accommodate the steamer from Leith. At the eastern end of Main Street, Scalloway Museum is an excellent place to study the origins of the fishing industry in the town and other aspects of local history. There is also a display on the history of the 'Shetland Bus'. During World War II Shetland was used as a base by the Norwegian resistance who ferried refugees from Norway to Shetland, in small fishing boats, returning with supplies and trained resistance fighters. Scalloway replaced Lunna House as their headquarters from 1942 as it had the necessary facilities to repair vessels damaged by German attack or winter storms. The museum focuses not just on surviving artefacts but on the people involved, both Shetlanders and Norwegians, many of whom make regular pilgrimages to the scene of their wartime exploits. It was a time of great bravery when many lives were lost. A book by their wartime commander, David Howarth, called *The Shetland Bus* details their exploits.

Across the road from the museum is the Old Haa of Scalloway dating from the middle of the eighteenth century. A plain, three-storey building now converted into flats, it has an armorial panel commemorating the marriage, in 1750 of James Scott to Katherine Sinclair, heiress of estates in Scalloway and Burra.

Top: The swimming pool at Scalloway, built with oil money – there is a pool in Shetland for every two thousand people
Above: The North Atlantic Fisheries College at Scalloway, where the next generation learn how to keep traditional industries alive

Examples of these haas (halls) occur all over Shetland. They were the houses of prosperous merchants or landowners and date from the seventeenth century onwards. They seem obtrusively tall buildings for such a windy climate but one explanation is that with a shortage of timber it was desirable to minimise the width of buildings and make abundant use of readily available stone.

SCALLOWAY CASTLE

Scalloway is dominated by its castle built, in 1600, by Earl Patrick Stewart. An inscription over the main door reads:

PATRICIVS STEVARDVS ORCHADIAE ET ZETLANDIAE
COMES. I. V. R. S.
CUJUS FVNDAMEN SAXVM EST DOM'ILLA MANEBIT
LABILIS E CONTRA SI SIT ARENA PERIT
A.D. 1600

Patrick Stewart, Earl of Orkney and Shetland. James V King of Scots.
That house whose foundation is rock will stand,
but will perish if it be shifting sand
AD 1600

The castle was built by local forced labour at a turbulent time in Shetland's history. When Earl Patrick Stewart succeeded his father as Earl of Orkney and Lord of Shetland in 1593, he determined to introduce Scots law and customs to Shetland and it was at this time that the law assembly, the lawting, was moved from Tingwall to Scalloway. Patrick Stewart ruled with an iron hand, tolerating no opposition to his plans and ambitions. He became immensely wealthy due to a combination of extortionate taxes, fines and confiscation of property. Earl Patrick Stewart only enjoyed Scalloway Castle and his new-found wealth until 1615 when he and his son were executed at Edinburgh for his excesses in Shetland and it soon fell into ruin.

Apart from a brief occupation by a Cromwellian garrison in the 1640s, the castle was never lived in after Patrick Stewart's downfall. It was a four-storey building with a stair tower and corner turrets. On the ground floor were the usual vaulted kitchens, storerooms and cellars, with the great hall on the floor above along with the earl's bedchamber. An impressive building, it failed to intimidate the locals. It has been under the care of the Secretary of State for Scotland since 1908 when the Marquis of Zetland gave it to the nation. Subsequently a programme of consolidation and restoration was put in hand and it is now well presented to visitors with interesting interpretative panels detailing its history and construction. Scalloway Castle was once surrounded by water on three sides with extensive outbuildings on the rest of the peninsula on which it stands.

Next door to the castle is the showroom of the Shetland Woollen Company, which is a good place to appreciate the traditional Shetland knitting industry. Now a multi-million pound export trade, it still relies on craft-knitters and many small-scale enterprises will catch the visitor's eye, all over Shetland.

TINGWALL LOCH

Above: Tingwall Loch, centre of several important sites from the Viking period

Right: The causeway leading to Ting Holm, submerged in the medieval period

ONLY A FEW MILES NORTH of Scalloway is Tingwall Loch which was the centre of the Norse administration of Shetland. Each district in Shetland had its area 'ting' or parliamentary assembly preserved in some of the district names such as Nesting, Aithsting, Delting, Lunnasting and so on. Once a year representatives of these assemblies met at the Law Ting Holm, at Tingwall (assembly valley), to pass laws and settle disputes which could not be agreed locally. A similar system of administration was introduced in other Norse areas and survives today in the Isle of Man and in Iceland. Most Hebridean islands, which were under Norse administration, had their own 'ting' sites and in some the sites of these survive in local traditions. In Easter Ross, the county town of Dingwall is another example of an assembly site in an area of Norse control.

49

Tingwall airstrip, near Lerwick, services the small islands of Fair Isle, Foula, Out Skerries and the northern isles of Yell and Unst

The Shetland site was originally on an island in the Loch of Tingwall, connected by a causeway to the loch shore. Again, this was a common arrangement in the Norse world. Indeed, the administrative centre of the Gaelic-Norse Lordship of the Isles, at Finlaggan in Islay, is located on a remarkably similar island site. In Shetland, a drop in the water level of the loch, combined with some silting, has left the causeway high and dry and access easy to the assembly site. An interpretative board beside the public road along the lochside gives an impression of what it might have looked like in Norse times. At the north end of Tingwall Loch is an ancient church, the most important pre-Reformation church in Shetland, underneath a replacement eighteenth-century building, and at the south end an even more ancient standing stone, hinting at an earlier ritual importance for this central area of Shetland.

Although Earl Patrick Stewart put an end to the Norse assemblies around 1600, Norse customs, and to some extent Norse laws and property rights, have survived to the present day. It is impossible to exaggerate the extent to which the Norse invaders took over Shetland life. This shows up particularly well in the place-name evidence where almost every settlement and landscape feature has a Norse name. A few names such as Pettaster, Pettifirth and Pettadale show residual signs of surviving Picts while Papil and Papa Stour preserve a memory of the Irish, Gaelic-speaking priests occupying remote monastic cells when the first Viking raiders arrived. Apart from the occasional English import, such as Bigton or Cunningsburgh, Norse names saturate the landscape.

Also at Tingwall is the seasonal Tingwall Agricultural Museum which is well worth a visit for the way it traces the evolution of farming practices and the introduction of mechanisation in the shape of many weird and wonderful contraptions.

The main road from Tingwall westwards passes Tingwall Airport from where tiny planes maintain a lifeline to the outlying islands of the Shetland archipelago. The road continues, much improved in recent years, winding over Wormadale Hill to Whiteness and Weisdale Voe. There are spectacular views down Whiteness Voe and from the road high above Weisdale Voe.

Just inland from Whiteness is the Loch of Strom, on which the ruins of Shetland's oldest castle occupy a tiny island, dating from around 1400. At the head of Weisdale Voe a minor road leads inland up a sheltered valley with a surprise at the end of it: plantations of trees at Kergord. This is the largest area of woodland in Shetland planted from the late nineteenth century onwards. Kergord House, built around 1850, was requisitioned as the administrative headquarters for the Scalloway-based Shetland Bus during World War II.

A Bronze Age standing stone at the south end of Tingwall Loch shows that this area was an important ritual centre in prehistoric times

TRONDRA AND WEST BURRA

Hamnavoe, on West Burra, is a picturesque and thriving community

TO THE SOUTH of Scalloway the main road crosses bridges built in 1971 to the islands of Trondra and West Burra. This is an especially attractive part of Shetland, and Hamnavoe, a tiny fishing village, is growing as Lerwick commuters prefer it to the comparative hustle and bustle of the capital. Hamnavoe developed as a fishing village and, by the twenties, was second only to Lerwick in importance. Its fleet now operates from the improved facilities at Scalloway but the village still houses many fishermen. Hamnavoe Primary School, built in 1980, has won awards for its architecture and design.

The crofter-fishermen in other parts of Shetland each had their own small boats, or combined in six-man boats called sixerns for fishing further afield. In Burra the fishing was so plentiful that the locals developed a four-man boat, the fourern, which they used to fish the Burra Haaf, a nearby offshore fishing ground. At first they sailed directly from the sandy beaches at the southern end of Burra but, as the fishing became more profitable, they invested in deeper-hulled vessels which used the harbour at Hamnavoe, built for the purpose.

Off to the west from above the little harbour at Hamnavoe there is a wonderful view to the island of Foula in the distance, with a scatter of smaller islands in the foreground, all uninhabited. One of these small islands, Papa, was presumably the site of an Early Christian monastery, as the name derives from the Norse *papae*, meaning 'priests', while the township of Papil, on West Burra has the same meaning. A stone from Papil, which once formed

Hamnavoe, on West Burra, is a picturesque and thriving community

PICTISH STONES

The dog-headed Pict on the Mail Stone is only the latest of many early carved slabs which have helped to round out our understanding of the Picts in Shetland. Other Pictish stones were found on St Ninian's Isle and in the parish of Lunnasting, bearing inscriptions in the Irish Ogham script. In this form of writing, vowels and consonants were indicated by lines and dots carved on the edges of squared stones. The Ogham inscriptions of Orkney and Shetland have proved impossible to translate and it has been suggested that the local Picts adapted the script to their own language. Another stone from Papil, a tall slab depicting a strange animal and more monks, is in the Royal Museum of Scotland in Edinburgh.

52

the side panel of a shrine, is in the Shetland Museum. It depicts a procession of monks holding croziers, and a monk on horseback, approaching a free-standing cross.

Trondra and the Burra isles are elongated and narrow islands, low-lying, and epitomise the flooded river-valley landscape which is so typical of Shetland. This is a fine area for walking expeditions with undemanding routes and attractive scenery all around. The views across from Burra to the west side of the Dunrossness peninsula emphasise the differences in fertility caused by the underlying geology. Kettla Ness, the most southern headland of West Burra, has a seabird colony. The headland is almost separated from the rest of the island and a beautiful sandy beach at this point is one of the finest on Shetland.

From the comparatively tranquil landscape of Trondra and the Burra isles we must now retrace our route northwards through Scalloway and Tingwall to Weisdale Voe, where the landscape changes dramatically as we enter the wilds of the Walls peninsula.

Weisdale is a fertile and sheltered valley, one of the very few areas in Shetland where people live out of sight of the sea

Left: Weisdale Mill, recently restored for use as an art gallery and exhibition centre

5 Walls and a Temple:
The Villages of West Mainland

REAWICK

The red sands of Reawick beach, caused by the old red sandstone, is a popular picnic spot with safe swimming. Reawick House, built in 1730 by the Umphreys after they had bought the Reawick estate from the Cheynes, is not improved by its red-tiled roof (added later). The castellated outbuildings have been described as 'toy forts'.

Beyond Skeld and Culswick, with its 1894 Methodist Chapel, is the deserted settlement of Sotersta with a scatter of ruined houses, a water mill and boat noosts on the beach. At the end of the beach, overlooking the entrance to Vaila Sound, is Culswick broch, ruinous by comparison with Mousa but still impressive with a height of 10ft (3m). The hollow-walled construction is clearly visible and an enormous triangular lintel in the entrance passage is impressive.

FROM WEISDALE VOE the road climbs uphill, giving fine views across the voe and over the scatter of islands to the south, towards Burra, then descends to the sea again at Tresta Voe. At Bixter the geology changes, as you cross the Walls Boundary Fault, into a landscape of old red sandstone with granite intrusions. A side road leads over the neck of the peninsula to Aith (Norse for isthmus). A series of minor roads leads to isolated settlements on the north coast of the Walls peninsula, while another road turns off to the south just west of Bixter, winding its way through the villages of Reawick and Skeld before turning north back to the main road. St Mary's chapel at Sand, down another side road before Reawick, was built in the twelfth century despite a local story that shipwrecked sailors from the Spanish Armada were responsible. (A good example of the unreliability of tradition, despite our predisposition to espouse the more romantic version!)

The Brig of Waas, leading to the district of Walls, a peninsula of scattered small communities

Previous page: Weisdale Voe, a fine example of a flooded river valley, now providing an interesting and distinctively Shetland landscape

STANYDALE

BEFORE REJOINING the main road at Brig of Waas, look for the turnoff to the Stanydale Temple. If you miss this turning, go back along the main road towards Bixter and follow the signs from there. Stanydale is unusual in Shetland as being one of the few places from where you cannot see the sea and it is possible that is *why* it is situated where it is! The site is reached by an easy walk across grassy moorland and is another quality site on an island group which has far more than its fair share of superb historic sites.

The Stanydale complex consists of a Neolithic settlement with the remains of houses, clearance cairns and field boundaries. It is not just an archaeological site, it is an archaeological landscape, of a type common throughout Britain but surviving in very few places. The largest building encloses an area 46ft (14m) by 33ft (10m) – too large to be considered as a typical Neolithic house which is why it has acquired the description of 'temple'. Perhaps 'meeting hall' would be a more appropriate, if less romantic, designation because it is clearly intended for some public use.

Stanydale Temple probably dates from 2500–2000BC from the period when the Neolithic settlers, the first farmers to reach Shetland, had spread throughout the British Isles. The wall of the structure was built from enormous boulders – hence the term 'megalithic' – it is 10–13ft (3–4m) thick. Two large postholes in the interior suggest a roofed structure, probably conical.

A feature of the structure is the series of recesses around the inner wall, reminiscent of bed-recesses in Neolithic houses but far too big for that purpose here. Outside the recesses were hearths suggesting that they may have been occupied, perhaps by family groups, during some tribal gathering. The excavators thought it was a temple, comparing it to structures in Neolithic and Bronze Age Malta, but modern experts fail to see more than a superficial resemblance. The authors of Historic Scotland's guide, *The Ancient Monuments of Shetland*, can only hedge their bets: '. . . perhaps Stanydale was a temple, perhaps a village hall, a meeting-house, or a courtroom. Perhaps it was all or none of these things. We may never know . . . '

WALLS

THE MAIN ROAD WEST crosses the Brig of Wass: turn left for the village of Walls (Waas), the main settlement of this district. The name is a corruption of the Norse *vaas*, meaning 'the place of voes'. The village is built round a fine natural harbour, popular with visiting yachts during the summer. Walls Museum is open by arrangement only. Bayhall House, another three-storeyed haa, was built around 1750 and converted to flats in 1978. To the west of Walls, Burrastow House, built in 1759, has been restored.

THE HAA OF SAND

The Haa of Sand, dating from 1754, is very similar to Scalloway Haa, also three storeys high and one room deep. It was built by Sir Andrew Mitchell of Westshore (Scalloway) as a summer house. He, apparently, was given permission by the Earl of Morton to remove dressed stones, lintels and two complete doorways from Scalloway Castle. It is an imposing building.

Top left: The prehistoric temple of Stanydale, well presented and interpreted for visitors, easily accessible despite its remote location in the middle of the Walls peninsula

Bottom left: The village of Walls with its shop and village hall is the centre of this western peninsula

Guarding the entrance to Walls harbour is the island of Vaila, with an important haa dating back to 1696, with late-Victorian additions. In 1893 it was sold to the Yorkshire mill owner, Herbert Anderton, who developed it as a summer residence. He fitted out a reconstructed boathouse as a Buddhist temple, since demolished, and entertained summer house-parties in a lavish style.

Side roads wind around back to the main road leading eventually to Sandness, a small village overlooking the Sound of Papa and the island of Papa Stour. Although there is a small pier below Sandness at Melby, the ferry for Papa Stour now leaves from West Burrafirth.

PAPA STOUR

PAPA STOUR, in Norse 'the big island of the priests', has a population of not much more than thirty, but a long history. There is an archaeological trail, fantastic cliff scenery, and fascinating historical yarns associated with some of the buildings. The simple kirk dates from 1806. Excavations at Biggings have revealed the foundations of a large medieval house while the ruins on top of the Maiden Stack, on the east side of the island, reputedly were used by a Norseman to imprison his daughter in order to preserve her virtue though love, or lust, triumphed and she was rescued by her young man. In the eighteenth century Papa Stour was used to isolate 'lepers' who, in fact, suffered from a hereditary and disfiguring skin disease. Locally available leaflets give more detail on the history and natural environment of Papa Stour.

Rejoining the mainland the countryside to the north of the main road is a maze of moorland and small lochs with endless opportunities for walking, trout-fishing and birdwatching. Many side roads lead through this maze to small townships such as Brindister, Clousta and Vementry. Vementry has a water mill with some machinery surviving in a roofless ruin. Vementry House, dating from the early years of the twentieth century, was possibly designed by the Edinburgh architect Sir Robert Lorimer who was a neighbour of its owner, Edmund Fraser. You can cross to the island of Vementry and explore over four thousand years of human history ranging from a Neolithic chambered cairn at Muckle Ward to World War 1 coastal defences, complete with guns, installed in 1917 to guard the anchorage at Swarback's Minn.

Two very different industries brought prosperity and expansion to the village of Aith: the knitting industry in which its women excelled; and whaling, which attracted a high proportion of its men.

Right: The island of Foula seen from the Walls area of west Mainland

6 OIL AND GRANITE:
North Mainland and Muckle Roe

WHALING

Whaling was an important feature of Shetland life but most Shetland men did their whaling either around Greenland or in the South Atlantic. Norwegian whaling stations were established on Shetland, after whaling was banned on the Norwegian coast in 1904, and the British Government gave permission to Norwegian companies to operate in Shetland. However, although it employed local people it was very unpopular with Shetlanders. Local fishermen feared the effect on the herring fishing while there were anti-whaling demonstrations because of the stench and pollution from the processing factories. Then, in 1908, Christian Salvesen & Co of Leith began operations in the Falkland Islands, and afterwards in South Georgia, employing two hundred Shetlanders a year between 1945 and 1963 and bringing about £200,000 a year into Shetland in wages. After 1963 it was no longer economically viable to operate in the Antarctic, and whaling ended.

NORTH OF LERWICK and Tingwall the main road north runs through the middle of Mainland, along a long glacial valley overlooked by the strange fingers of Mid Kames and East Kames, skirting the district of Nesting and Lunnasting in East Mainland. These are distinctive districts, a bit off the beaten track, but with plenty of charm and plenty of interest. The ferry for Whalsay leaves from Laxo at the head of Dury Voe, while the ferry for Out Skerries sails from Vidlin, a little further north. There is a good view of Vidlin Voe from the road along its eastern side from where a minor road branches off to Lunnin Head once a thriving settlement but now occupied by only two or three families. There are prehistoric houses on Lunnin Head, from where there is a fantastic view over the Lunna peninsula to Fetlar, Yell and Fedeland to the north and to Whalsay and Out Skerries to the east. Vidlin House dates from the eighteenth century but is much altered.

Above: The settlement of Brae, located on a narrow neck of land between Sullom Voe to the north and Olna Firth to the south

Overleaf: The settlement of Voe, at the head of Olna Firth, has a distinctly Scandinavian appearance

From the crossroads at Vidlin a road runs north up the Lunna peninsula which is almost cut in two by the sea at the site of Lunna Kirk and Lunna House. Lunna Kirk, built in 1753 but dedicated to St Margaret and possibly on the site of an earlier chapel, is one of the most attractive in Shetland with an original interior and an interesting churchyard. It contains a much-photographed tree and simple memorial stones to Norwegian resistance fighters lost on the Shetland Bus which, for a while, used the nearby Lunna House, dating from 1660, as its headquarters before moving to Scalloway. On the shore is a fishing booth, now roofless, and between it and the church you cross the course of the Ninian pipeline heading for Sullom Voe.

Abandoning your vehicle at Outrabister House, at the end of the public road, there is an excellent walk to the headland of Lunna Ness, a glacial landscape showing signs of ice scratches on many boulders and outcrops. The Stanes of Stofast are large glacial erratics – a fascinating area for geologists.

Back on the main road north, just before the settlement of Voe at the head of Olna Firth, another road branches off to the north into the district of Delting. This is the main route for the ferries to the northern islands of Yell, Unst and Fetlar. As the route climbs high above Dales Voe there is a fine view of Fora Ness and the twin Ayres of Swinister where gravel and sand tombolos connect it to the mainland.

The village of Voe itself is another 'Scandinavian' settlement, its colourfully painted houses recalling Norwegian fjord settlements. In the nineteenth century it was an important centre for cod fishing , while on the north side of Olna Firth a whaling station operated from 1904 to 1928.

On the narrow neck of land between Olna Firth and Sullom Voe is the scattered townships of Brae and Burravoe, a prosperous looking settlement, with a brand new swimming pool, school and community centre. The village expanded during the construction phase of the Sullom Voe oil terminal, as the village is at the crossroads for the road north to the terminal.

SULLOM VOE

THERE IS NOT MUCH for the passing tourist to see at Sullom Voe and, in fact, the best views are from the west side of the voe, from the road to Punds. It is not possible for unauthorised personnel to gain access to the oil terminal. It is the largest oil and liquefied gas terminal in Europe, processing around one million barrels of crude oil every day. Supertankers load here and transport oil from the Brent and Ninian oil fields all over the world. Safety is taken very seriously and, so far, there have been only minor oil spillages. The flare stacks are more impressive at night but, in general, the complex makes a gratifyingly small impact on the landscape. The terminal was begun in 1973 and completed in 1982, employing more than six thousand men in the construction phase. The terminal has its own airstrip, Scatsta, which was used during World War II.

Top left: Vidlin Voe, Lunnasting: a sheltered ferry terminal serving Out Skerries

Bottom left: The largest oil terminal in Europe, at Sullom Voe, merges into the Shetland landscape

HILLSWICK

Hillswick claims Shetland's oldest public house, the Booth, dating from 1698. Adolf Westerman, a Hamburg merchant, had a booth here in 1684. Hillswick has always been popular with tourists because of the spectacular coastal scenery between here and Esha Ness. At one time it was the northern terminus of the West Side steamer service which encouraged tourists to visit. It was once possible to sail direct to Hillswick from Leith, the port for Edinburgh. St Magnus Hotel was built around 1900 for cruise passengers by the North of Scotland, Orkney & Shetland Steam Navigation Co Ltd. It is a timber building, imported from Norway, with decorative gable trusses in 'Swiss' style.

Top right: Mavis Grind, where the waters of the North Sea and the North Atlantic almost cut off the Northmaven district of Shetland's Mainland

Bottom right: A Bronze Age standing stone near the settlement of Brae, Delting

MUCKLE ROE

JUST PAST the village of Brae a road turns south for Busta, where there is an excellent country house hotel, and Muckle Roe, an island now connected to the mainland by a bridge. Busta House dates from 1714 and was the home of the Gifford family. Parts of the house may date from the sixteenth century.

The road north crosses Mavis Grind, in Norse meaning 'the gate of the narrow isthmus'. It is only a few yards from the North Sea, on one side, to the Atlantic Ocean, on the other. The road in this sector has been massively improved in recent years but has lost some of its charm. A road sign on the isthmus warns drivers to beware of otters crossing the road. There is a good view of the narrow isthmus and the surrounding countryside from the hill to the north, reached by a quarry road.

North of Mavis Grind the main road divides with the left fork leading to Hillswick and Esha Ness and the right fork leading to North Roe and Fedeland. This is the district of Northmaven, again quite distinct from other parts of Shetland, yet another example of why the Shetland Isles are such an interesting place to visit. Northmaven is one of the most desolate and infertile parts of Shetland though there are small pockets of arable land along its east coast, and elsewhere. The underlying geology is a reddish-pink granite, and diorite, with areas of old red sandstone and gneiss. The line of the Walls Boundary Fault defines the eastern coastline of the area to the north of Mavis Grind.

Along the southern coast of Esha Ness are a series of coastal villages, each attractive and with constantly changing views of the dramatic sea stacks and natural arches which attract visitors to the area. At Tangwick Haa, built in the eighteenth century, a small museum explains the local history. There are good views of the Drongs and Dore Holm from Tangwick.

Esha Ness itself has amazing black basalt cliff scenery and a lighthouse, built in 1929. There are good interpretative boards beside the lighthouse which explain the local geology and the natural environment. There are also archaeological sites in the area and good walks and trails make this an interesting place to spend an afternoon.

On the north side of Esha Ness Rønas Voe and Orr Wick separate it from the lands to the north which are dominated by the granite bulk of Rønas Hill. Just to the north of Collafirth a road runs inland up to the summit of Collafirth Hill where there are communication masts and an abandoned military base. From there it is an easy walk to the summit of Rønas Hill where there is a Neolithic cairn. The views, even from Collafirth Hill, are far-ranging and unforgettable.

North of Rønas Hill is a true wilderness of small lochs and moorland, a tremendous place for walking and exploring, as long as you have a good map. The main road runs up the east side of North Mainland, passing the

villages at Ollaberry, Lochend and North Roe. Ollaberry was formerly a fishing station and has a fine nineteenth-century pier. Former fishing booths at the head of the pier have been converted into houses. Ollaberry Haa, built in 1789, was restored in 1972.

Beyond North Roe and Isbister there are further marvellous walks to Fedeland. This is an extremely interesting little peninsula for geologists, while the wildlife and cliff scenery is equally appealing. North of the Point of Fedeland are the jagged Ramna Stacks, a seabird metropolis in the breeding season. At Sandvoe there is a fine sandy beach while, to the west, along the coast geologists have identified the oldest rocks in Shetland, over 2,000 million years old.

There are other important seabird breeding colonies on the little islands scattered in Yell Sound and on the cliffs of the west side of Yell (the best views of which are from the North Mainland Road).

We have reached, at Fedeland, the most northerly point of the Mainland of Shetland but further north are the northern isles of Yell, Unst and Fetlar, each with its own character and appeal. To reach these islands we must retrace our steps past Mavis Grind and Brae to Voe and take the road north to the ferry terminal at Toft, in the district of Delting.

Above: Basalt lava cliff scenery at Esha Ness, near the lighthouse

Top left: Peat banks, Esha Ness

Bottom left: A good view of Rønas Hill, from the south side of Rønas Voe

71

7 Shetland's Northern Isles:
Whalsay, Unst, Yell and Fetlar

WHALSAY

THE ISLAND OF WHALSAY lies about 3 miles (5km) east of the Mainland of Shetland, and is about 5 miles (8km) long by 2 miles (3km) wide, aligned in a NE–SW direction. The ferry departs from Laxo in the Lunnasting district of North Mainland from where there is an excellent and frequent service to Symbister. The crossing takes thirty minutes and is remarkably cheap compared to similar services elsewhere in the British Isles. The population of Whalsay, at the 1991 Census, was 1,043 and it has a reputation for prosperity based on the modern fishing fleet at Symbister which is the island's main settlement. The name is derived from the Norse for 'whale island' probably because of its shape when seen from the sea.

The Pier House at Symbister harbour is a restored Hanseatic böd, or booth, now housing a display explaining how German merchants traded with Shetland in the Middle Ages until the Union of Scotland and England in 1707 brought an end to this enterprise. Shetlanders traded salted and dried fish for alcohol, tobacco, cloth and salt. The Pier House also displays material on the history of Whalsay. The Pier House is a tiny, two-storey building with a hoist for loading and unloading ships. Some of the nearby buildings along the waterfront date from the seventeenth century.

Above: The lowland Scots poet Hugh MacDiarmid lived here on Whalsay

Left: The Pier House at Symbister, a restored Hanseatic Böd, used by German merchants from the Middle Ages to the early eighteenth century

Detail of wall of the Pier House, Symbister, Whalsay

The new Whalsay Leisure Centre and swimming pool, by contrast, is a modern, well-designed, architecturally appealing building, beside the new school. With over one thousand people on such a small island, there is lots going on and the community centre is well used. Although life on the island is dominated by fishing there is also some crofting and traditional activities such as peat-cutting are still carried on. A road runs for almost the full length of the island along the west coast as far as Skaw where there are standing stones. The township of Brough, and the broch which gives it its name, lie about half way up the island on the west side. From there, a road crosses to the east side, to Isbister, passing fine examples of planticrubs on the way. These are tiny drystone enclosures which were used in cultivating seedlings, giving them protection from the wind. They can be both square and round.

To the north of Isbister are prehistoric houses, over four thousand years old. From this side of the island there is a good view to the Out Skerries although from this distance it is hard to imagine that the few low-lying scraps of land on the horizon could support human settlement.

From Isbister the road loops back to Symbister, passing the township of Sodom (in Norse, *Sudheim*, meaning the southern part of the original Norse settlement). Here, the Scottish poet and essayist Hugh MacDiarmid (C. M. Grieve) lived with his wife and child from 1933 to 1942, living the simple life before his reputation brought him economic security at least in small measure.

SYMBISTER HOUSE

Above the town is Symbister House, an elegant Georgian mansion, ruined in the forties when it was converted into the island's school. The conversion was truly hideous and has to be seen to be believed. It would be wonderful if the authorities responsible for its desecration could restore Symbister House to its former glory but this seems unlikely. Behind the mansion are stables, offices, coach houses and outbuildings in a state of decay. It was built in 1823 by Robert Bruce of Symbister using grey granite from Nesting.

YELL

THE ISLAND OF YELL is reached by the short ferry crossing from Toft, near Sullom Voe, to Ulsta at the south end of Yell. It probably takes its name from the Norse *gall*, barren: in the sagas it is referred to as *Jala*. Yell is the largest of the Northern Isles and is indeed a peat-covered and infertile place with the exception of a few favoured pockets. It is 17 miles (27km) from north to south and up to 5 miles (8km) wide, although almost cut in two in the middle by sea lochs running far inland from both sides. The population at the 1991 census was 1,083.

The main route north out of Ulsta passes the Ness of Sound double tombolo, a fine example of this distinctively Shetland coastal feature. The road passes abandoned settlements then crosses the island to Mid Yell, the island's main community. The old churchyard, overlooking the harbour, contains the ruins of an earlier church replaced in 1832 by St John's Kirk. The Yell Leisure Centre, built in 1988, has a leisure pool and sports hall in a building of interesting design, yet another example of oil money benefitting Shetland's far-flung communities. Mid Yell is also the home of the renowned Shetland naturalist and ornithologist, Bobby Tulloch.

From Mid Yell a minor road returns down the east coast of the island over moorland to Aywick and Burravoe where the island's oldest building,

Top left: Peat-cutting, Whalsay

Bottom left: Cullivoe, Yell, looking across to the cliffs of Unst

Overleaf: An old fishing station at Gloup on the north coast of the island of Yell

The lighthouse on Muckle Flugga, the most northerly scrap of the United Kingdom

the Old Haa of Brough, is situated. Built in 1672, it overlooks the entrance into Burravoe. Before the modern road was widened all traffic had to pass through an archway which connected the main house to cottages opposite. It is an extremely attractive building, harled in gleaming white, and contains a museum and interpretation of the island's history and natural environment. In front of the haa is the propeller of a Catalina aircraft which crashed above the village during World War II. Leaflets give good information on local history and on walks around the island.

The Burravoe road continues back to Ulsta completing a loop round the southern half of the island. North of Mid Yell, the main road runs through Sellafirth to Gutcher, which is the ferry terminal for both Unst and Fetlar, but it is well worth while to take the time to continue to the north coast of Yell, through Cullivoe and Greenbank, to Gloup. There, the elegant eighteenth-century Gloup Haa has been restored. Gloup was an important

fishing station in the nineteenth century and remains of the fish-processing site can be seen. Overlooking it is the Gloup Memorial, commemorating fifty-eight men who were drowned in July 1881, when a sudden storm wrecked six fishing boats, Some find the memorial unduly sentimental and perhaps it would be even more moving if it were displayed to better effect. There are some fine coastal walks around Gloup Voe.

Returning to Gutcher, there are frequent ferry crossings to Unst, the next island to the north. The crossing takes ten minutes.

UNST

THE ISLAND OF UNST is the most northerly of the Shetland Isles. It has a similar rectangular shape to that of Yell, but is smaller, measuring 12 miles (19km) from north to south by 5 miles (8km) across. The population at the 1991 Census was 1,067. The ferry arrives at Belmont where the mansion house, from which the village takes its name, was built in 1777. The house was built by Thomas Mouat who toured the Lowlands for ideas before deciding on this design.

Geologically speaking Unst is appealing with bands of serpentine, once mined commercially. A fault line runs down the middle of the island forming a line of weakness now occupied by Burra Firth and the Loch of Cliff.

The main road north leads to Baltasound, about half-way up the eastern side of the island. From the 1880s until the 1920s this was one of Shetland's chief herring ports. The island's airstrip is located on the south side of the sound. Further north is Haroldswick and its Post Office, distinguished by its fire-engine red colour, is the most northerly one in the British Isles. The Unst Leisure Centre, at Clibberswick, has an accumulation of material relating to the history and environment of the island. Nearby is RAF housing and administrative blocks, servicing the dramatically sited commu-

LIGHT ON THE ROCKS

Muckle Flugga lighthouse, completed in 1858, was designed by David and Thomas Stevenson. It sits, perched, on what is no more than a large rock with a short tower with the lantern on top and an accommodation block for three keepers below.

The most northerly Post Office in the British Isles, at Haroldswick, Unst

Overleaf: Red, white and blue at Norwick, on the north-east corner of Unst

nications base on Saxa Vord. Access is restricted but, from a road giving access to local people to peat cuttings on the slopes of Saxa Vord, there is a fine view of the final scraps of land in the British Isles, Muckle Flugga with its lighthouse and Out Stack just beyond. Alternatively, you can drive from Haroldswick across to Burrafirth and then walk up the Hermaness peninsula – an outstanding excursion. Hermaness National Nature Reserve is regarded as being of international importance. Walking in this area requires good footwear, and a good head for heights, but the cliff scenery is well worth the effort. There are large breeding colonies of seabirds on the cliffs, which reach a height of 558ft (170m), including the largest colony of puffins on Shetland.

It is worth driving past Haroldswick to Norwick and Skaw. At Norwick there is a stunningly beautiful beach from where the road climbs steeply and onwards to Skaw, the most northerly house in the British Isles (not counting Muckle Flugga).

Returning to the south end of Unst, a road leads from Uyeasound across to Muness where there is an outstanding castle – not surprisingly the most northerly castle in the British Isles. Built in 1598 by Laurence Bruce of Cultmalindie in Perthshire, at the suggestion of his half-brother Robert Stewart, he instituted a regime every bit as cruel. Muness Castle was probably designed by the same man who built the castle at Scalloway, Andrew Crawford. The castle lasted a little longer than Scalloway as a residence, but had fallen out of use within a century. Above the entrance is a panel with an inscription in late Gothic letters:

Coat of arms and inscription panel, Muness Castle, Unst

LIST ZE TO KNAW YIS BULDING QUHA BEGAN
LAURENCE THE BRUCE HE WAS THAT WORTHY MAN
QUHA ERNESTLY HIS AIRIS AND OFSPRING PRAYIS
TO HELP AND NOT TO HURT THIS VARK ALUAYIS
THE ZEIR OF GOD 1598

Muness Castle, and the adjoining farm buildings, are very photogenic, and much admired by visitors.

On the road back to Uyeasound, stop and admire one of the finest standing stones in Shetland, just beside the road. From this spot there is a fine view to Fetlar and the many small islands offshore. Erected in the Bronze Age, when the weather was better and observing conditions much superior, it is thought that standing stones like this one were used in astronomical calculations (if not to assist eclipse prediction then at least to establish the exact days of midsummer and midwinter).

Returning to Belmont, or Gutcher on Yell, it is possible to connect with the ferry service to Fetlar.

Top left: Muness Castle, Unst, built in 1598 by Laurence Bruce

Bottom left: The most northerly house in the United Kingdom, at Skaw, Unst

Overleaf: Cliff scenery on the north coast of Unst

FETLAR

VISITING FETLAR on the same day as a visit to Yell and Unst is possible, but not recommended, because although it is a very small island it deserves enough time to explore it properly and to appreciate its distinctive features. Fetlar lies to the south of Unst, and is only 5 miles (8km) by 2.5 miles (4km), with a population of under one hundred. At one time it supported over nine hundred people and, indeed, its Norse name means 'fat land' in recognition of its fertility. Geologically it is similar to the southern part of Unst but is renowned for the variety of pebbles on its shingle beaches.

The RSPB North Fetlar Reserve is restricted during the summer months and should not be approached without consulting the warden. A heritage centre at Houbie explains the human and natural history of the island and sells local crafts.

Just south of the ferry terminal at Oddsta is Brough Lodge. Built around 1820 for Arthur Nicolson of Lochend, who had bought most of Fetlar from the Bruces, it is Gothic in style but carried to the extreme. It is now a decaying ruin without many redeeming features.

The main fishing station on Fetlar was on the east coast of the island at Funzie (pronounced Finnie). Here the road ends but it is worth walking on to the north-east corner of the island to see the remains of a monastic settlement at Strandibrough.

There are several quite substantial houses on the island, and the T-plan manse, built in 1756 is unusual. It is in a favoured location surrounded by trees. Fetlar Kirk, built in 1790, is quite narrow with round-headed windows and a belfry.

Booklets on the history of the Northern Isles and leaflets detailing walks and visitor attractions are available from the Tourist Information Office in Lerwick and from local museums, shops and heritage centres. Shetland is particularly well organised from the point of view of visitor information, both in the printed form and in the form of interpretative panels at major monuments. In this respect it contrasts greatly with its Hebridean neighbours to the south. The series of books on walking the coastline of Shetland is especially good.

ANCIENT HISTORY

Fetlar has an interesting range of archaeological monuments. There is a Neolithic chambered cairn at Vord Hill and a very thin Bronze Age standing stone, known as the Ripple Stone, at Leagarth, in front of Leagarth House. The Giant's Grave at Aith is possibly a Norse burial site. In the middle of the island, at Hjaltadans, there is a ring of large stones encircling two central stones. According to local tradition, these represent a fiddler and his wife trapped in a ring of petrified trolls.

An imposing Bronze Age standing stone near Muness, Unst

8 SHETLAND'S REMOTER ISLANDS:
Out Skerries, Foula and Fair Isle

OUT SKERRIES

SHETLAND'S OUT SKERRIES are a few rocky islands amounting to only 600 acres (243ha) about 5 miles (8km) north-east of Whalsay and about 10 miles (16km) east of the Shetland Mainland. The small car ferry sails from either Vidlin, in East Mainland, or from Lerwick. There is also an airstrip. It is possible to visit Out Skerries for the day, spending a few hours there, which is just enough to begin to understand what life is like there. There are not many places like it anywhere else in the British Isles.

The two main islands are Housay and Bruray, often called East Isle and West Isle, connected in 1957 by a road bridge replacing an earlier foot bridge. The islands form a natural harbour protecting the fishing fleet of three boats. The island of Grunay is privately owned. The Out Skerries lighthouse guards the entrance to the harbour and warns mariners to stay clear. Built in 1857 by David and Thomas Stevenson, it has not prevented shipwrecks in more recent times.

The cliff scenery is enhanced by natural arches and blow-holes. The rocks are gneiss and schist with a band of limestone, providing some fertility to the soil, though most of the population of eighty-seven make their living from the sea.

Even on these remote scraps of land there is evidence of prehistoric settlement, in the form of a circle of stones, with a diameter of 43ft (13m) thought to date from the Bronze Age, at Battle Pund.

The island school covers both primary and secondary age groups and, with only two teachers, is easily Britain's smallest secondary school. Modern communications have removed the precarious element of life on the Out Skerries, but, in winter storm conditions, these can be disrupted.

FOULA

FOULA is the most westerly of the Shetland Islands, lying 14 miles (23km) west of the nearest point on the Shetland Mainland. An air service connects the island to Tingwall Airport while the ferry operates from Walls. As the ferry boat is based at Foula, day-trips are not possible except if arriving by air.

It is thought that the name, pronounced Fool-a, derives from the Norse *Fugl ey*, meaning 'bird island'. It is 3.5 miles (5.6km) by 2.5 miles (4km) with a population of around forty human beings and several thousand seabirds. Foula has precipitous sea-cliffs, mostly of banded sandstones, reaching a height at the Kame of 1,220ft (372m) surpassed in Britain only by the cliffs of St Kilda, an even more isolated outpost lying to the west of the Hebrides. The highest point of the island is the Sneug, at 1,370ft (418m). The population is concentrated either at Ham, around the recently improved harbour, or at Hametoun in the south of the island.

ROMAN THULE?

The profile of Foula is visible from far away and may have been noted by the Romans. When the Roman fleet sailed around Britain in around AD82-85, it made contact with the inhabitants of the Orkney Islands and according to Tacitus: '. . . dispecta est et Thule.' – Thule too was seen. As only Fair Isle, Fitful Head and Foula are visible from Orkney, it seems likely that Foula's distinctive shape was seen by the Romans.

The main sources of income for the resident population are sheep and crofting, lobster and crab fishing, tourism, spinning and weaving and the sale of knitwear, sheepskin rugs and other crafts. Fishing is the mainstay of the island economy between April and September, after which the boats have to be lifted ashore for safety.

Traces of prehistoric occupation are evident and the island came under Norse control along with the rest of Shetland. There may have been a monastic cell on the Priest's Stack at the north side of Foula. The people of Foula still celebrate Christmas on 6th January and New Year's Day on 13th January, adhering to the old Julian calendar which was replaced in the rest of Britain by the Gregorian calendar in 1752.

The island has a famous shipwreck, the *Oceanic*, (a sister ship of the *Titanic*) which proved equally sinkable when it hit a reef off Foula in 1914.

Overlooking the harbour is a small eighteenth-century haa, a plain house built for the Scotts of Melby with an unfinished baronial porch stuck unhappily to its front.

FAIR ISLE

FAIR ISLE lies 24 miles (39km) south-west of Sumburgh Head in Shetland and 27 miles (43km) north-east of North Ronaldsay in Orkney. Administratively it is part of Shetland. It is 3 miles (5km) from north to south and 1.5 miles (2.5km) wide, surrounded by towering cliffs except at the Haven and at the south end. The name derives from the Norse *Fridarey* meaning 'the peaceful isle'. There is an airstrip on the island and a ferry based there. The purpose-built *Good Shepherd IV*, constructed in 1986, makes the $2^1/_2$ hour trip to Grutness, near Sumburgh Airport. Since 1954, Fair Isle has belonged to the National Trust for Scotland.

Most visitors are interested in the birdlife and make for the Fair Isle Lodge and Bird Observatory. A new building was erected in 1969 and refurbished twenty years later with excellent research facilities. Fair Isle is a staging post for migrant birds: over 340 species have been recorded. There are also seventeen species of seabirds breeding on Fair Isle.

There are traces of prehistoric settlement dating as far back as the Neolithic period, and the remains of an Iron Age fort. An enormous burnt mound, 128ft (39m) by 89ft (27m) standing 10ft (3m) high, is the largest in Shetland.

The George Waterston Memorial Centre commemorates the man who conceived the idea of a bird observatory on Fair Isle while held as a German prisoner-of-war. He had visited the island in 1935 and, in 1948, bought the island and started to put his plans into action. The centre has a museum of island history. The population of Fair Isle at the 1991 Census was only 68, compared to 380 in the middle of the nineteenth century. One hundred and thirty-seven islanders were forced to emigrate in 1862.

There is a haa house on Fair Isle, dating from the eighteenth century, where the novelist Walter Scott was entertained in 1814.

Left: Foula, from Esha Ness

SHIPWRECKED

Many ships have come to grief on the rocky coasts of Fair Isle, despite a lighthouse at each end of the island, built in 1891. There were no lighthouses in 1588 when El Gran Grifon, a troop ship in the Spanish Armada, was wrecked on Fair Isle with three hundred soldiers aboard with an almost devastating effect on the islanders. Folklore connects the famous Fair Isle knitting patterns with the Spanish influences but, in fact, a Norse origin is far more likely. In 1868 the German emigrant ship Lessing was wrecked here but all 465 people on board were saved by the islanders.

Overleaf: Twin black sheep on Burra Isle, south of Scalloway

9 Walks and Excursions

ACCESS

BEFORE DESCRIBING some possibilities for walking excursions on the islands of Shetland, a brief word about rights of access. Basically, access (on foot) to the countryside in Shetland, and to all historic sites, is unrestricted, bounded only by considerations of courtesy and common sense. It is sensible to ask directions, if not permission. Any advice offered should be followed, and visitors should take particular care not to damage dykes and fences, and to avoid disturbing stock, especially in the lambing season. Even the sight of an unfamiliar dog can upset sheep, so visitors should keep their pets well away from sheep, or at the very least under close control, preferably on a leash.

Freedom of access does not give visitors the right to tamper with historic sites without the owner's permission. Similarly, visitors must apply to the appropriate authorities for permits to fish. Hotels and the Tourist Information Centre in Lerwick can offer advice about where to apply. Although there are no laws prohibiting rights of access, there has to be some give and take with landowners and farmers. Their livelihood is often at stake, as well as other people's jobs.

Above: The P&O ferry St Sunniva *heading up the Sound of Bressay for the voyage to Aberdeen*

Left: A photogenic fishing boat at Uyea Sound, Unst

Overleaf: The roofless ruin of Scalloway castle, once the most impressive building in Scotland

EQUIPMENT

VISITORS ALWAYS HOPE for good weather, but in our climate there are no guarantees, only wishful thinking, and in the absence of a direct line to the Almighty certain precautions are essential. The key elements in Shetland's weather are wetness and wind. Even when the sky is blue and the hill-lochs are shimmering with scenic beauty, the ground underfoot is likely to be boggy once off roads and tracks. Adequate raingear and correct footwear will make it possible to have a good time, whatever the weather. Inadequate protection leads inevitably to saturation, cold, misery, recriminations and regret, especially where small children are concerned. Wet clothing can be dried out – eventually – but without doubt prevention is the best cure. Even on a fine day there is likely to be a brisk breeze, and light, windproof jackets or anoraks should always be carried. The weather can change quickly, often with little warning, and although inadequately clad walkers are unlikely to come to any harm, they can certainly become exceedingly miserable very quickly.

Correct footwear is most important. Proper walking boots with Vibram soles are best, and need not be expensive or heavy. Good walking shoes are acceptable only for farm tracks or beachcombing expeditions. Trainers will become soaked in anything but drought conditions and can be ruined quickly and easily. Wellies are uncomfortable to walk in for any distance, and are positively dangerous in wet conditions. If you buy new boots or shoes for your island adventure, try to break them in first, or come well-provided with plasters to deal with the inevitable blisters.

Walking in Shetland is, for the most part, straightforward and easy, with good tracks and pathways. It is a well-populated landscape, with few places far from human habitation. The main danger for walkers is on the cliffs, where the desire for a better viewpoint of nesting seabirds can easily lead the unaware into danger. It is especially dangerous for children in these areas.

COLLAFIRTH HILL – RØNAS HILL
2 – 3 HOURS

MANY VISITORS will be attracted by the idea of climbing Shetland's highest hill, in the Northmavine district of Mainland. Rønas Hill, at a height of 1,475ft (450m), is modest by Scottish standards, but it is an interesting walk with a rewarding view. From the main road at the bottom of the Ministry of Defence road up Collafirth Hill it is about a three-hour round trip walk to the summit of Rønas Hill. Alternatively you can drive to the radio masts at the top of Collafirth Hill and park there, from where it is a two-hour round trip to the top of Rønas Hill.

HILLTOP BURIAL

The trig point at the top of Rønas Hill is protected by a modern cairn of stones and boulders, but just to its west is one which is far more ancient, a prehistoric burial cairn. Almost certainly this dates to the time of the Neolithic first farmers, and has been there for some 5,000 years. The implications of this cairn for an understanding of Neolithic society are clear: it is a long way from fertile pastures and fields to this barren summit, and yet the prehistoric folk felt that it was important and significant to bury their tribal leaders here. The cairn is well preserved, its burial chamber reached through an entrance passage. The chamber itself is built of massive blocks and is rectangular: 4ft high, 5ft 6in long and 3ft wide (1.2m x 1.67m x 0.90m), with the entrance passage in the middle of the eastern side of the rectangle. The entrance faces to the east, to the rising sun, as is so often the case in cairns of this period. Some of the kerbstones surrounding the circular cairn survive, and for those interested in archaeology this is an amazing site, especially in its spectacular situation.

Neolithic cairns are thought to have been communal tribal graves, perhaps reserved for the ruling family, and used over a period of many centuries. Shetland cairns of this period are heel-shaped, with a slightly concave façade on each side of the entrance, presumably with a courtyard in front where ceremonies were performed.

This is a weird landscape, of shattered pink granite boulders strewn everywhere, through which a pink track winds westwards from the old army signals unit concrete buildings on Collafirth Hill. It is worth savouring the view to the east from Collafirth Hill before moving on. The best views are from the bends on the approach road before the summit plateau of Collafirth Hill is reached: far down below is Colla Firth, from which the hill gets its name, opening up into Yell Sound, scattered with tiny islands, with the bulk of the island of Yell behind. To the south is Sullom Voe, with the narrows of Mavis Grind and Brae clearly visible.

Pressing on across the pink boulder field, the route is due west up the gentle eastern slopes of Rønas Hill to the white Ordnance Survey trig point on the summit. This is a barren landscape, with just a few tufts of grass – here we are above the heather line, and it is indeed a true subarctic wilderness. The route to the summit can be made even easier by avoiding the stream between Collafirth Hill and Rønas Hill. This is Grud Burn, which flows out of a small round hill-loch or tarn. By walking to the north of this puddle in the granite it is easy to walk up the gentle northern ridge of Rønas Hill to the summit.

The view from the top of Rønas Hill is spectacular: the immediate surrounds are pink granite, stretching in all directions; to the south is Rønas Voe and Esha Ness, with the whole of the Shetland Isles stretching out towards Fair Isle in the far distance; to the north is the strange landscape of Northmavine (sometimes spelled Northmaven), with dozens of hill lochs in an eroded landscape, a true wilderness maze. One of the lochs, Pettadale Water, hints at the presence of Picts in this area when the Viking invaders arrived – 'pett' or 'pit' in a place-name is evidence of a Pictish farmstead in the vicinity. Far off to the north-east the lighthouse on Muckle Flugga, north of the most northerly point of the island of Unst, can sometimes be seen.

Many Shetlanders – and visitors – find this is a suitable place to celebrate midsummer sunset on the longest day of the year, so if you want to experience something of the emotion that caused our Neolithic ancestors to use this summit for rituals of their own, you could think about joining in. However, if you value the isolation – and desolation – of this place, pick some other day.

The more adventurous walkers may wish to head north-west of Rønas Hill, following the Burn of Monius down to Ketligill Head, passing the remains of possibly prehistoric buildings on the way. At Ketligill Head climb down to the Lang Ayre, a long sandy beach reddened by the local granite. Offshore are sea stacks, spectacular in their natural architecture. Gruna Stack, with its natural buttresses, has been likened to a cathedral.

It is certainly well worthwhile continuing up the coast to the bay of Lang Clodie Wick, where two waterfalls run off the plateau above the cliffs, returning through the watery maze north of Rønas Hill to the Collafirth Hill road.

Left: Not a modern example of a Viking boat burial, but an example of recycling in a society where this has been normal for thousands of years

ISBISTER – FEDELAND
2 HOURS

THE PROMONTORY OF FEDELAND (sometimes also spelled Fethaland) is the most northerly point of the Mainland of Shetland and a favourite destination for island walkers. Visitors will find it particularly interesting too, its geology, natural history, archaeology, coastal scenery and settlement history unrivalled for such a small area, even in Shetland.

The geology is complex, attracting students and amateur geologists. West of Sandvoe can be found examples of gneiss, over 2,000 million years old, the oldest rocks in Europe. From the Viking farmstead of Isbister, still a farmhouse, a path leads up the middle of the peninsula to Fedeland, although the longer route around the coast above Sandvoe is more rewarding. No dogs are allowed in this area.

It is worth climbing to the top of Brunt Hill for the panoramic view. To the west is the island of Øya (Uyea), to the north the Ramna Stacks, an RSPB reserve and major breeding colony for seabirds. They were once used as a bombing range but are protected now. To the east the island of Yell dominates, but far to the north-east the hill of Saxa Vord on Unst can be seen. To the south the pink granite mound of Rønas Hill is prominent.

Fedeland itself was once one of the busiest places on Shetland, between the beginning of June and the middle of August: this was the haaf fishing season, and there was a fishing station here, where fish landed at Øya, as well as those landed locally, were dried and prepared for export. It is completely deserted now, but the ruins of over twenty buildings hint at the hustle and bustle – as well as the workers at the fishing station, the crews of over sixty six-man boats (sixerns) were based here during the short fishing season.

On the south-east side of the narrow isthmus connecting the 'island' of Fedeland to the Mainland are two good examples of boat 'noosts' – protective stone settings used from Viking times up to recent times. On the green plateau above them is a prehistoric homestead, perhaps dating from the Iron Age, but conceivably much older.

On the coast there are outcrops of steatite, a soft rock sometimes called 'soapstone' from which bowls and urns were carved in prehistoric times. Following the coastline south there is much of interest: ancient sites, deserted houses and settlements, wonderful coastal scenery. The Kame of Isbister, a promontory surmounted by a grassy plateau, contains the remains of over twenty buildings. It may be a monastic settlement, dating from Pictish times, perhaps established by Irish monks. There is a similar site on the west coast of Yell at Birrier, directly opposite.

The cliff scenery of Fedeland is spectacular, exhilarating, visually exciting – and dangerous. Please be careful!

Left: Traditional Scottish burgh architecture in Scalloway, near the medieval castle

Overleaf: Not very impressive now, this island castle in the Loch of Strom, north of Scalloway, was an important fortress in the Middle Ages

99

GLOUP FISHING STATION, YELL

A VISIT to the old fishing station at Gloup, on the north coast of the island of Yell, involves a long, full-day excursion from Lerwick, and a very short walk. From Lerwick drive north, turning off the main road at Voe, following the signs for the Yell and Unst ferries. There is a frequent service from Toft, near Sullom Voe, to Ulsta, at the south-western corner of Yell. From Ulsta, drive north through West Sandwick and Mid-Yell to Sellafirth, turning north just before the Gutcher ferry terminal (ferry for Unst). The road passes through the townships of Cullivoe and Greenbank, before turning west and terminating at Gloup.

Park the car and follow the signs to the Gloup memorial. This is a large stone slab on which are inscribed the names of fifty-eight men drowned on the night of 20/21st July 1881, with the names of their fishing boats, where known. Above the memorial is a statue of a mother and child, representing one of the thirty-four widows and eighty-five fatherless children left by the tragedy.

In the nineteenth century Gloup was one of the busiest fishing stations in Shetland. The boats from the area – known as 'sixerns' or 'sixereens' because they were crewed by six men – used to travel to the 'far haaf', the deep-sea fishing forty miles and more from land, where cod and ling were caught during the summer fishing season; these were landed at the nearest fishing station, where they were dried and packed for export. Summer storms occasionally wrought havoc amongst the fishing fleet. For example, in 1832 thirty-one north Mainland boats were lost, at a cost of 105 lives. The fifty-eight men commemorated at Gloup came from ten boats, mostly from the immediate area; this was a devastating tragedy in a small community. The memorial was erected in 1981 and dedicated on the hundredth anniversary of the disaster.

On the shore below the Gloup memorial is the site of the fishing station, of which little now remains. The sea, and the fishing, have been part of the history and culture of Shetland for hundreds of years. The export trade in salted fish began in the fourteenth century, trading with the merchants of the Hanseatic League who rented böds (booths) at fishing ports in which they carried out their trade. Whitefish, mainly cod and ling, were traded for nets, fine cloth, wines and luxury goods, often in bartering. The Pier House at Whalsay was a Hanseatic booth, and the small exhibition there explains the history of that trade and its importance to the Shetland economy. The introduction of a salt tax in 1712 by the British Government effectively ended this chapter in Shetland's economic history.

In the sixteenth century Dutch fishermen began to venture into northern waters, fishing for herring. In the eighteenth century the reorganisation of Shetland's tenancies and the arrival of Scottish landowners who created new estates, created a situation in which fishing was linked to rents in a most direct way, often forcing men to put to sea in dangerous or

Top left: Lunna Kirk, with Lunna House in the background – headquarters for Norwegian resistance fighters during World War II

Bottom left: A deserted village in Lunna Ness

Fora Ness, Delting: an island linked to the mainland by two gravel spits or ayres

marginal conditions. There were many minor tragedies, as well as the devastating disasters such as the one remembered at Gloup.

From 1820 larger fishing smacks began to fish for cod, ranging far and wide across the North Atlantic. The cod were cleaned and salted on board to preserve them, returned to Shetland, dried, and exported all over the world. From the 1870s Shetlanders developed a herring fishery – later than in the Western Isles, for example – which grew rapidly in the early years of the twentieth century. Herring were landed at the fish factories at Lerwick and Bressay, processed and packed in barrels for export. Local girls and women worked as gutters. In 1905 there were 174 herring stations throughout Shetland, which produced over one million barrels of herring for export, mainly to Europe. After 1920 the herring fishery collapsed throughout Scotland, for reasons not completely understood. It is possible that the stocks were over fished, causing a catastrophic decline. In modern times Shetland's fishing fleet, much reduced in numbers, uses the latest technology to bring prosperity to those still working in the industry, which is still one of the most dangerous and insecure ways of earning a living. Fish farming, especially for salmon, is well suited to Shetland's sheltered voes and firths, though after initial economic success competition from Norwegian fish farms threatens the very existence of this new industry.

Beside the Gloup memorial is the old Haa of Gloup, recently renovated. At the end of the road, at Kirks, is the site of a medieval chapel and graveyard.

This excursion can be extended to include a visit to the island of Unst, crossing by ferry from Gutcher to Belmont, though in one day there is barely enough time to see more of Unst than lies adjacent to the main road. However, a visit to Skaw, the most northerly house in Britain, to Haroldswick, with the most northerly post office, and to Muness, the most northerly castle, can easily be fitted in.

SKAW–LAMBA NESS–NORWICK, UNST
1½– 2 HOURS

IT IS POSSIBLE to drive to Skaw, the most northerly house in the British Isles, parking opposite the Haa of Skaw. Continue on foot to the beach at the Wick of Skaw, where more boat noosts can be found. In the sand dunes, prehistoric round houses have yielded stone tools and could easily date from the Neolithic period; perhaps there is the possibility of several periods of occupation here – excavations in the 1970s seemed to show different phases. It is worth climbing the headland on the north side of the Wick of Skaw for a view of the Holm of Skaw, a small offshore island formerly used for grazing sheep. Inland from Skaw there is a small valley, which seems to have traces of agriculture and settlement going back at least as far as the Bronze Age.

It is well worth walking back to Norwick by way of the peninsula of Lamba Ness, easily identified by the radio masts used to communicate with the oil fields to the east of Shetland. At the point of Lamba Ness overlooking Cudda Stack is an excellent place to watch seabirds. In February 1936 the Leith trawler *May Island* was wrecked here with all hands lost.

Returning along the path along the southern edge of the peninsula, look for Saxa's Kettle. This is a sea stack at the base of which the sea flows through a tunnel into a circular rock basin which 'comes to the boil' during a gale. Saxi may have been a Norse settler, though in Shetland tradition he is a mythical giant, also commemorated in the name of the nearby hill, Saxa Vord, now also the name of an RAF base. There are local legends about trolls on the top of Saxa Vord, on which there were ancient ruins before the communication antennae took over the site.

After rejoining the Skaw road you descend steeply to the north end of the bay of Nor Wick. The houses there have one of the finest views in Shetland and are amongst the most picturesque. While descending the road, enjoy the views across the bay to the cliffs of Burgar. Walk along the beach at Norwick, noting the Taing (Norse: 'tongue'), a promontory jutting out into the sea. Iron Age pottery was found here in the 1970s. At the end of the beach turn inland to the medieval chapel of Kirkaton, of which only the foundations remain, with its burial ground; many of the gravestones are very ancient. The church here is dedicated to St John. Beside it is the modern war memorial, and the village of Norwick, a very lively community where many Shetland traditions are still observed.

MAPS AND GUIDES

The Tourist Information Centre at Lerwick, the Shetland Times bookshop there, local shops throughout Shetland, and the many local museums and heritage centres all sell locally-produced guidebooks, booklets and leaflets, including an excellent series entitled Walking the Coastline of Shetland. Many of these outlets also supply the maps without which any walk in Shetland will be less well appreciated. The 1:50,000 Ordnance Survey 'Landranger' maps are adequate for general orientation and planning excursions, but the 1:25,000 'Pathfinder' maps are necessary if you are off the beaten track. There are many parts of Shetland well away from main roads where it is easy to lose direction if the mist descends quickly – which is by no means unusual, even in summer, and good maps, along with good equipment and emergency supplies, should be in every rucksack.

FURTHER POSSIBILITIES

THESE FEW WALKS and excursions hopefully give a hint of the possibilities for exploring Shetland on foot. The use of a car is a big advantage, but the public transport system can easily be used. Shetlanders are great walkers, and a few enquiries at your hotel or B & B, or in the local shop, will bring directions and advice about favourite local haunts. As the road system on Shetland improves, even on the remoter islands, there is more of a temptation to stay in the car and explore by road in order to see as much as possible in the time available. But if you never get out of your car and leave the road behind you, you will miss the magic of Shetland. At Esha Ness there are interpretation panels and ideas for exploring the area on foot, and we have mentioned the Neolithic 'temple' at Stanydale, Walls, which involves a short walk across a landscape which has hardly changed in the last 5,000 years. In the south of Shetland the wreck of the *Braer* has brought visitors to the coast south of Quendale, although with every year that passes there is less and less to see. The smaller islands of Papa Stour, Fetlar, Bressay, Foula and Fair Isle are best explored on foot – in some cases there is no alternative. Many can easily be visited in a day, or even in half of a day. Even Lerwick is best explored on foot, leaving the car in the large car park at the old harbour.

The wildlife, the wild flowers and the archaeology make for interesting walks and excursions, but the ever-changing views of sea-coast and sky are what makes the landscape of Shetland different from anywhere else in the world. The fresh air, wind and rain are addictive to visitors, and even if Shetlanders feel that there is often too much of them, they miss them when they leave the islands, as so many of them do. The changing patterns of weather, the long summer days and the long winter nights, and the landscape they love, are what they talk about when in exile. The visitor who is privileged to experience this place, even for a short time, will surely understand just a little why Shetlanders feel this way.

The Tourist Information Centre, Lerwick, provides comprehensive information on accommodation and holiday opportunities throughout Shetland

Shetland's fast inter-island ferries provide an excellent communications link between the outlying islands and the Shetland Mainland

USEFUL INFORMATION AND PLACES TO VISIT

TOURIST INFORMATION

Shetland Islands Tourism
Market Cross, Lerwick, Shetland, ZE1 0LU
Tel: 01595 693434 Fax: 01595 695807

Tourist Information Centre
Market Cross, Lerwick, Shetland, ZE1 0LU
Tel: 01595 693434; Fax: 01595 695775

TRAVEL

British Airways, Sumburgh Airport, Tel: 01950 460345

Inter-Island Ferries: Booking Offices
Yell, Unst, Fetlar	Tel: 01957 722259
Whalsay	Tel: 01806 566259
Out Skerries	Tel: 01806 515226
Fair Isle	Tel: 01595 760222
Foula	Tel: 01595 810460
Papa Stour	Tel: 01595 873227

Loganair, Tingwall Airport, Tel: 01595 540246

P & O Scottish Ferries
Holmsgarth Ferry Terminal, Lerwick, Tel: 01595 694848

P & O Scottish Ferries
Jamieson's Quay, Aberdeen, AB9 8DL, Tel: 01224 572615

Shalder Coaches Limited
Lower Scord, Scalloway, Shetland, ZE1 0UQ
Tel: 01595 880217

PLACES TO VISIT

Böd of Gremista Museum, Lerwick
Open June to August, 10.00–13.00, 14.00–17.00 Wed–Sun

Clickimin Broch, Lerwick
Located on west edge of the town

Dim Riv, Lerwick Harbour
Trips around the harbour in replica of Viking longship, summer evenings.
Tel: 01595 693434 (Tourist Information Centre) for bookings and information

Fort Charlotte, Lerwick
Built 1665, with later additions. Good views of harbour

George Waterston Memorial Centre, Fair Isle
Museum of island life, history, folklore;
Open by arrangement. Tel: 01595 760244

Jarlshof Prehistoric Village, Viking and Medieval Settlement
Located near Sumburgh Airport, open all year: April to September, 09.30–18.30 Mon–Sat; 14.00–18.30 Sun: Entry to small museum and exhibition. October to March: admission to grounds only.

Mousa Broch
Located on island of Mousa
Tel: 01950 431361 to book boat trip

Old Haa, Burravoe, Yell
Open April to September, 10.00–16.00, and by arrangement. Tel: 01957 722339

Quendale Mill, Dunrossness
Working mill and museum.
Tel: 01950 460422 for information

Scalloway Castle, Scalloway
Open all year: 09.30–19.00 Mon–Sat; 14.00–19.00 Sun. Admission free.

Scalloway Museum, Main Street, Scalloway
Open May to September, 14.00–17.00 Sun, Tues, Wed, Thurs; 10.00–13.00, 14.00–17.00, Sat.
Tel: 01595 880256 or 880675

Shetland Croft House Museum, Voe, Dunrossness
Open June to September, 10.00–13.00, 14.00–17.00, daily except Mon.

Shetland Library, Lower Hillhead, Lerwick
The Shetland Room contains a wealth of local history material. Tel: 01595 693868

Shetland Museum, Lower Hillhead, Lerwick
Open all year: 10.00–19.00 Mon, Wed, Fri; 10.00–17.00 Tues, Thurs, Sat. Admission free.
Tel: 01595 695057

Tangwick Haa, Esha Ness
History of Northmavine in restored 'haa' house: Open May to October, 14.00–18.00 Mon–Fri; 11.00–19.00 Sat–Sun

The Pier House, Symbister, Whalsay
Restored Hanseatic booth with exhibition
Open 9.00–13.00, 14.00–17.00, Mon to Sat; 14.00–16.00 Sun. Key available from Bremen Café or 'Harbour View'

Tingwall Agricultural Museum, Gott
Working croft and farming museum.
Open May to September, 10.00–13.00, 14.00–17.00.
Tues, Thurs, Sat or by arrangement. Tel: 01595 840344

Unst Heritage Centre, Haroldswick, Unst
Museum of island history: Open May, 14.00–16.00 Sat and Sun; June and September, 14.00–16.00 Tues, Wed, Sat and Sun; July and August, daily 14.00–17.00
Tel: 01957 711510 or 711667

Up Helly Aa Exhibition, St Sunniva Street, Lerwick
Display of Viking longship and photos of annual January fire festival

Weisdale Mill, Textile Museum and Art Gallery
Working museum, café. Tel: 01595 830400 for information and opening times

For information on hired cars, chartered boats, outdoor activities, swimming pools and leisure facilities, accommodation and restaurants, contact the Tourist Information Centre, Lerwick, where there is also an excellent selection of information on the complete range of activities available to visitors.

PLACE NAMES AND THEIR INTERPRETATION

Balta Sound	N. *balti-ey*	Balti's island sound
Bixter	N. *bygg-setr*	barley farm
Brae	N. *breid eid*	broad isthmus
Bressay	N. *Brus-ey*	Brusi's island
Burra	N. *borgar-fjord*	fort firth
Busta	N. *bolstadr*	farmstead
Cardwell	N. *Korti-völlr*	Korti's field
Clickimin	N. *klakk-minni*	rock mouth
Cunningsburgh	N. *konungr-byr*	king's dwelling
Delting	N. *dal-thing*	assembly valley
Drongs	N. *drangr*	pointed rocks
Dunrossness	N. *dynr-rost-nes*	headland of the din, noise of the whirlpool
Eshaness	N. *esja-nes*	soapstone headland
Fair Isle	N. *faer*	sheep
Fetlar	N. *fetlar*	belts, straps
Fitful Head	N. *fitfugl*	web-footed bird
Foula	N. *fugl-ay*	sea-fowl island
Hannavoe	N. *hafnar-vagr*	harbour bay
Haroldswick	N. *Haralds-vik*	Harald's bay
Hillswick	N. *Hildis-vik*	Halldor's (?) bay
Isbister	N. *austr-bolstadr*	easterly homestead
Laxa	N. *lax-ay*	salmon island
Laxford	N. *lax-fjord*	salmon firth
Laxvoe	N. *lax-vagr*	salmon bay
Lerwick	N. *leir-vik*	mud bay
Loch of Spiggie	N. *spigg*	stickleback loch
Lunnasting	N. *lundr-eid-thing*	grove-isthmus-assembly place
Mainland	N. *megin-land*	chief land

Mavis Grind	N.	*maef-eid grind*	gate of the narrow isthmus
Mousa	N.	*mose-a*	moss island
Nesting	N.	*nes-thing*	headland of the assembly
Ollaberry	N.	*Olafs-borg*	Olaf's fort, township
Papa Stour	N.	*pap-ey stor*	great priest-island
Petta Water	Pictish	*pit*	Pict's piece of land
Quarff	N.	*hvarf*	a turning, shelter
Quendale	N.	*kvan-dalr*	wife-valley
Rønas voe	N.	*raudr-nes vagr*	red headland bay
Sandsting	N.	*sand-thing*	assembly on the sands
Sandwick	N.	*sand-vik*	sandy bay
Scalloway	N.	*skala-vagr*	creek, bay with sheds, huts
Shetland	N.	*Hjaltland*	sword-hilt land
Skelda Ness	N.	*skelda-nes*	headland of the shelter island
Sullom Voe	N.	*sule-heimr vagr*	home of the gannets bay
Sumburgh	N.	*Svin-borgr*	Sween's fort
Symbister	N.	*sunn-bolstadr*	southerly homestead
Tingwall	N.	*thing-vollr*	assembly meeting place
Unst	N.	*örn(?)-vist*	eagle's dwelling
Uyea Sound	N.	*öyja*	island sound
Vidlin	N.	*vidr-land*	wide grove
Voe	N.	*vagr*	bay, creek
Walls	N.	*vagar*	bays, creeks
Weisdale	N.	*ves(?)-dal*	dale of the mansion
Whalsay	N.	*hvals-ey*	whale's island
Yell	N.	*geldr*	barren

N – Norse

FURTHER READING

Cluness, A. T. *The Shetland Isles* (Hale, 1951)

Finnie, Mike *Shetland: An Illustrated Architectural Guide* (RIAS, 1990)

Fojut, Noel and Pringle, Denys *The Ancient Monuments of Shetland* (HMSO, 1993)

Howarth, David *The Shetland Bus* (London, 1951)

Jakobsen, Jakob *The Place-names of Shetland* (1936; reprinted 1993)

Knox, Susan A. *The Making of the Shetland Landscape* (John Donald, 1985)

Lunnasting Primary School *The Tullochs and the Braer Disaster* (1993)

Malcolm, D. *Shetland's Wild Flowers* (Shetland Times, 1992)

Nicolson, James R. *Shetland* (David & Charles, 1984)

Nicolson, James R. *Traditional Life in Shetland* (London, 1978)

Schei, Liv and Moberg, Gunnie *The Shetland Story* (Batsford, 1988)

Shetland Islands Tourism *Shetland: Official Tourist Guide* (1994)

Smith, Brian (ed), *Shetland Documents, 1580–1611 (Shetland Times, 1994)*

Smith, Hance D. *Shetland Life and Trade, 1550 – 1914* (John Donald, 1984)

Tulloch, Bobby *A Guide to Shetland's Breeding Birds* (Shetland Times, 1992)

Tulloch, Bobby *Bobby Tulloch's Shetland* (Shetland Times, 1993)

Wills, Jonathan and Warner, Karen *Innocent Passage: the Wreck of the Tanker Braer* (Mainstream, 1993)

Wills, Jonathan *A Place in the Sun: Shetland and Oil–Myths and Realities* (Mainstream, 1991)

Withrington, Donald J. (ed) *Shetland and the Outside World, 1469–1969* (University of Aberdeen, 1983)

Most of these books have extensive bibliographies for those wishing to pursue research in more depth. In addition, there are many booklets and pamphlets covering all aspects of Shetland: walks, islands, birds, knitting, historic sites, landscapes.

INDEX

Page numbers in *italic* indicate illustrations

Access, 93
Airports, 24, 42, 50, *50*, 79, 87, 89, 107
Anderson, Arthur, 28
Archives, 28
Area, 8

Baltasound, 79
Belmont, 79
Birds, *12*, 14–15, *14*, 15, 33, 42, 71
Böd of Gremista, 28, 107
Brae, *66*, 67, *69*
Braer, 13, 42, 106
Bressay, 27, 31, 33, *93*
Brig of Waas, *56–7*
Brochs, 20–1, 28, *29*, *35*, *38*, 39, 42, 57
Bronze Age, 19–20, 42–3, 50
Burra Isle, *90–1*
Burravoe, 75, 78
Bus services, *18*, 107

Caithness, 8
Castles, *45*, 50, *82*, 83, *83*, *94*
Clibberswick, 79
Clickimin broch, 28, *29*, 107
Clickimin Leisure Centre, 28
Climate, 19–20
Collafirth Hill, 95, 97
Crofting, 39–41
Cullivoe, *4–5*, *74*

Dunrossness, 35, 39

Equipment, 95
Esha Ness, 68, *70*, 107

Fair Isle, 89
Farming, 39–41
Faroes, 8
Fedeland, 71, 99
Ferry services, 7–8, *22–3*, 24, 28, 33, *33*, 63, *63*, 67, 73, 75, 79, 85, 87, 89, *93*, *106*, 107
Fetlar, 85
Fiddle music, 31

Fishing, 33, 45, 63, 67, 78–9, 85, 89, 103–4
Fladdabister, 39
Footwear, 95
Fora Ness, *104*
Fort Charlotte, 27, 107
Foula, *61*, 87, *88*

Geology, 13–14, 33, 53, 57, 67–8, 71, 79, 87, 99
Gloup, *75–6*, 78–9, 103–4
Gulberwick, 39

Haa houses, 39, 46, 59, 68, 71, 78, 89
Hamnavoe, 51, *51*
Haroldswick, 79, *79*
Hermaness, 83
Hillswick, 68

Ice Age, 13
Iceland, 8
Identity, 44
Irish monks, 21, 51, 60, 99

Jarlshof, *41*, 42–3, *43*, *44*, 107

Kergord, 50
Knab, 31
Knitting industry, 47, 60

Landscape, 7, 28, 53
Latitude, 7
Lerwick, 7, *7*, 8, *8*, 9, *18*, 24, *26*, 27–8, 31, *31*
Library, 27–8, 107
Lifeboat, *33*
Lighthouses, *22–3*, 31, 42, 68, *78*, 79, 87, 89
Loch of Spiggie, 42
Loch of Strom, 50, *100–1*
Lodberries, 8, 27–8
Lunna House, *21*, 67, *102*
Lunna Kirk, *16–17*, 67, *102*
Lunna Ness, *102*

Lunnin, *13*, *15*

MacDiarmid, Hugh, *73*, 75
Mail stone, 39
Maps, 105
Mavis Grind, 68, *68*
Midsummer day, 8, 97
Mid Yell, 75
Mousa broch, 21, 28, *35*, *38*, 107
Muckle Flugga, *78*, 79, 83
Muness Castle, *82*, 83, *83*
Museums, *15*, 27–8, 33, 39, 42, 46, 107

Neolithic settlers, 19, 42, 95
Norse administration, 48
Norse settlers, 9, 21, 42–4
North Atlantic Fisheries College, *46*
North Sea oil, 24, 28, 39
Norway, 8
Norwick, *80–1*, 105
Noss, *12*, 33

Old Haa of Brough, 78, 107
Olna Firth, *63–4*
Orkney, 8, 21
Otters, 15
Out Skerries, 63, 75, *86*, 87

Papa Stour, 60
Peat, 19–20, *70*, *74*
Picts, 21, 28, 33, 39, 40, 42, 50, 51, 97, 99
Pier House, Symbister, *72*, 73, *73*, 107
Place-names, 108–9
Plants, 19
Population, 9, 27, 33, 35, 45, 73, 75, 79, 87, 89

Quendale Mill, 42, 107

Reawick, 57
Recycling, *96*
Rønas Hill, 14, *70*, 71, 95, 97

Sandwick, *34*, *36–7*, 39

Saxa Vord, 83, 105
Scalloway, 27, 45–7, *98*, 107
Scalloway Castle, 47, *94*, 107
Scott, Sir Walter, 43
Seals, 19, 39
Shetland 'Bus', *21*, 46, 50, 67
Shetland Croft Museum, *15*, 39, 41, 107
Shetland ponies, 15, 33
Skaw, *82*, 83, 105
Sovereignty, 21, 43
Spanish Armada, 57, 89
Standing stones, 19–20, *50*, *69*, 83, 85, *85*, 87
Stanydale Temple, *58*
Stewart, Patrick, 24, 47, 50
Stewart, Robert, 42
St Ninian's Isle, 13, 28, 40
Sullom Voe, 13, *66*, 67
Sumburgh Airport, 24, 42
Sumburgh Head, 14, 42
Submburgh Hotel, *40–1*, 42

Swimming pools, 28, *46*, 67, 75
Symbister, 73, 75
Symbister House, 75

Thule, 87
Ting Holm, 48, *49*
Tingwall Agricultural Museum, 50, 107
Tingwall Loch, *48–9*, 50
Tombolos, *10–11*, 40, 67
Tourism, 13, 68
Tourist Information Centre, 24, 31, 93, 105, *106*
Treaty of Perth (1266), 21
Trondra, 51

Unst, *4–5*, *74*, 79, *80–2*, *84*, *92*
Up Helly Aa, 31, 107
Uyea Sound, *92*
Uyeasound, 83

Vaila, 60

Vementry, 60
Vidlin, 67
Vidlin House, 63
Vidlin Voe, *66*
Viking galleys, 8, 31
Vikings, 8, 21
Voe, *64–5*, 67
Voes, 13

Walls, 57, *58*, 59–60
Waterston, George, 89
Weisdale, *52–3*
Weisdale Mill, *52*, 107
Weisdale Voe, *54–5*
West Burra, 51, *51*
Whaling, 60, 63
Whalsay, 73
Wheelhouses, 21, 42, *44*

Yachts, *18*, 24
Yell, *4–5*, *10–11*, 13, *74*, 75